Architecting the Future Enterprise

Architecting the Future Enterprise

Deborah J. Nightingale and Donna H. Rhodes

The MIT Press
Cambridge, Massachusetts
London, England

MIT Press books may be purchased at special quantity discounts for business or sales promotional use. For information, please email special_sales@mitpress.mit.edu.

This book was set in ITC Stone Serif by Toppan Best-set Premedia Limited, Hong Kong. Printed and bound in the United States of America.

Library of Congress Cataloging-in-Publication Data.
Nightingale, Deborah J.
  Architecting the future enterprise / Deborah J. Nightingale and Donna H. Rhodes.
    pages cm
  Includes bibliographical references and index.
  ISBN 978-0-262-02882-0 (hardcover : alk. paper) 1. Business enterprises. I. Rhodes, Donna H. II. Title.
  HD2351.N54 2015
  658—dc23
                                        2014029656

10 9 8 7 6 5 4 3 2 1

Contents

Preface

In this ever-changing world, enterprises of all shapes and sizes are under constant pressure to innovate and transform in order to stay viable. *Architecting the Future Enterprise* is about creating the "blueprint" for what the enterprise will look like in the future, after a transformation vision is realized.

Our Motivation

The subject of this book is a framework for undertaking a significant endeavor in order to evolve an existing enterprise, or to design a new one. Our *ARIES framework* has its origins in our prior experiences and in our research on enterprises as systems. We have personally led enterprise transformation efforts and served in industry leadership positions in enterprises undergoing major change. We have researched and observed underlying theory and applied enterprise transformation.

More than a decade ago, we decided that there was a significant gap in the existing enterprise transformation theory and practice. This gap was the failure to adequately apply architecting as the initial phase in the transformation life-cycle. We recognize the accomplishments and continuing progress in the development of enterprise architecture frameworks, yet we concluded and continue to believe that these are insufficient. This motivated us to undertake a significant research endeavor in our ongoing research program at the Massachusetts Institute of Technology.

Existing architecture frameworks are highly useful in what we would call the design phase. Our work is targeted upstream from that phase, in the early concept phase. Just as systems, hardware, and software engineering found the need to establish architecting as a unique activity within engineering, enterprises require the same. Modern enterprises are increasingly complex and interconnected. Architecting is necessary to make the "(re)engineering of enterprises" tractable.

Influences

Our work has been influenced by many insightful publications and individuals too numerous to identify individually. A number of key thinkers in the areas of systems and enterprises have had a powerful impact on how we think about enterprises, and on why we believe architecting is so important to the field of enterprise science. We include notes throughout the book to highlight some individuals, books, and papers.

Many colleagues in industry and government have helped shape our understanding of enterprises and the challenges that must be overcome. They are individuals we have worked with in our respective industry careers, in our education and research careers, and through our involvement in professional societies. These include partners in other research programs around the world, as well as the executives we have worked with—and learned from—in education settings, in research, and in consulting engagements. Our work has been influenced by numerous colleagues in the Institute of Industrial Engineers (IIE) and the International Council on Systems Engineering (INCOSE).

At MIT, many colleagues and students have influenced our work on enterprises. These include (but are not limited to) colleagues from the Engineering Systems Division, the Lean Advancement (formerly Aerospace) Initiative, the Sociotechnical Systems Research Center, and the Systems Engineering Advancement Research Initiative.

Organization of This Book

The eleven chapters of our book tell a story, from start to finish, about architecting the future enterprise. In chapter 1, we describe the motivation for our work, and how we believe it adds to the already significant body of knowledge on the art and practice of transforming an enterprise. In chapter 2, we present the ARIES (Architecting Innovative Enterprise Strategy) framework, including our ten–enterprise element model and our architecting process model.

The next three chapters concern enterprises as they presently exist. Chapters 3 and 4 focus on the larger ecosystem of an enterprise and on stakeholder value—today and for the future. In chapter 5, we outline an approach for capturing an understanding of the current enterprise, as relevant to the enterprise's strategic imperatives for change.

Creating a holistic vision for the future enterprise is the subject of chapter 6. We discuss the use of vivid descriptions, stakeholder vignettes, and narratives told through the various lenses of our ten-element model.

Chapter 7 covers our approach to generating concepts and developing alternative architectures—in other words, discovering what is possible for a future architecture. Chapter 8, on the process and techniques for evaluating these possible architectures, focuses on the difficult decision of choosing the future architecture.

In chapter 9, we present a technique for checking alignment in the future architecture. We discuss implementation planning as well as communicating the new architecture to stakeholders.

Chapter 10 tells the story of a recent enterprise architecting project. While every architecting endeavor is unique, this chapter provides a sense of how the ARIES framework is used in real-world practice to produce a blueprint for the future.

Chapter 11 presents our seven architecting imperatives: the fundamentals we believe should be part of every enterprise transformation project, regardless of the specific framework or techniques used.

Throughout the book we incorporate examples from many of the enterprise architecting projects we have been involved in. At the end of chapters 3 through 9, we include suggested exercises and questions for consideration, which you can apply to your enterprise to enhance your understanding of the material in the book. Finally, two appendixes are included at the end of the book, to provide executive summaries of two additional architecting projects.

Acknowledgments

We would like to acknowledge the many graduate students who have participated in our classes and research programs, too numerous to call out individually. They have had a major role in what we have achieved and in shaping the material presented in this book. Many of their contributions made through graduate thesis work are referenced within.

We would also like to sincerely acknowledge the colleagues who spent time reviewing our materials and providing invaluable input and suggestions for improvement. In particular, we would like to acknowledge Mark Prendergast for his creative graphics and help in developing other materials over the past several years.

We also extend a special thanks to our former doctoral student, Caroline Lamb, who worked with us in the early stages of organizing our materials for the book.

Finally, we would like to thank our family and friends for their encouragement and patience throughout this process.

1 Why Architecting Matters

The beginning is the most important part of the work.
—Plato

It is no surprise that enterprises[1] that fail to keep up with the changing world around them are sooner or later doomed to failure. This is precisely why enterprises periodically undertake planned transformations. What is surprising is just how many enterprises falter, and perhaps even fail to survive, in spite of determined efforts to undertake the necessary change.

The process of transforming an enterprise is not simple. There can be all sorts of known and unknown pitfalls throughout the entire journey, but we can say one thing for certain: a transformation initiative that does not begin well is not likely to end well. The question, then, is "How do we begin well?"

There are many types of enterprises—corporations, government agencies, start-ups, nonprofits, and universities, to name only a few—but we believe all enterprises share four fundamental characteristics. First, an enterprise consists of people who generate value for others, by producing a product and/or performing a service of some kind. Second, an enterprise is a *whole system* that has a purpose, a "reason for being."[2] This purpose is evident in the enterprise's strategy, stated or implied; it's a way of doing things (e.g., processes, procedures, knowledge), a way of organizing, a culture (e.g., a belief system, trust, openness), and a way to measure itself (e.g., profits, societal benefits). Third, an enterprise benefits from being part of its larger *ecosystem,* the living environment in which it exists and operates. Fourth, every enterprise must periodically undergo transformation as it evolves and adapts to an ever-changing world.[3]

Why Enterprises Transform

Enterprises are continually evolving. This may be driven by changing needs, desired growth, or new opportunities and threats to existence (e.g., new technologies, market shifts, and workforce shortages).[4] Most often, changing the enterprise involves small adjustments in strategy, organization, processes, or infrastructure. Transformations, on the other hand, result in significant change. These may be deliberately undertaken when things are just not working as they should, particularly as time goes on and the world surrounding the enterprise changes. Acquisitions and mergers almost always trigger change. Transformations are also undertaken for purely strategic reasons, such as desired business growth or market expansion.

Transformations generally involve making tough choices with incomplete information, and sound early decisions are critical. Some enterprise transformation initiatives are designed to implement strategic changes in direction. Perhaps the enterprise wants to enter a new market or alter its business model, or maybe it wants to extend its offerings from products alone, to both products and services. Or it might be a long-term transition from a domestic business base to a global one.

A transformation effort may be triggered by a disruptive event or rapidly changing circumstances. For instance, the sudden emergence of a major competitor might make the enterprise's current product line appear less attractive to customers. Or maybe an unanticipated change in trade policy suddenly creates the opportunity to do business in a new region.

The same types of transformations—an acquisition, for example—can occur through long-term planning or be triggered by a disruptive circumstance. Consider an enterprise seeking to acquire a firm as part of its long-term growth plan. This would necessitate adjustments in the newly combined enterprise in some manner, and this is most likely already part of the overall acquisition plan. A disruptive event, like the sudden opportunity to make an unplanned acquisition, perhaps because of another firm's financial difficulties, also requires action. In this case, the necessary transformation is unanticipated.

Whether anticipated or not, transformations in enterprises occur in cycles. When anticipated, transformation likely aligns with the larger strategic cycles of the enterprise. Unanticipated transformations have cycles that align with timescales of an emergent need or a window of opportunity. If it is a multiyear effort, some parts of the enterprise implementing change are likely to align with normal strategic planning cycles.

Successful transformation, we believe, starts with taking a holistic approach to creating the blueprint for change as the initial activity. We call this activity *architecting the future enterprise*. To understand what we mean by holistic, it is helpful to examine problems associated with the opposite tactic—what could be called a reductionist or piecemeal approach. All sorts of failures can result when the focus is on a single aspect (e.g., technology, organization) without taking

Table 1.1

Enterprise architecting failure types and impacts

When in doubt, reorganize	Reorganizing can be disruptive when performed in isolation, with failure to achieve targeted outcomes.
Forgetting stakeholders	Inadequate stakeholder analysis can lead to decisions that are misaligned with what stakeholders need and expect from the enterprise.
It is all about technology	Expensive technology applications frequently address only a portion of the strategic issues and often fail in isolation.
Silo effects	Silo implementations almost always create fiefdoms and suboptimize the enterprise by failing to consider other parts of the organization.
Information technology will fix everything	Focusing on IT without considering other elements frequently leads to expensive failures.

into account the whole. Let's examine some of these failures to gain insight into what happens when one fails to consider the whole enterprise from the start.

Five Architecting Failures

We have observed many types of architecting failures in our studies of enterprises, and have encountered many stories in the literature of things gone wrong. So what are some of these potential failures? Table 1.1 summarizes five failure types with a simple statement of the impact of each failure on the enterprise.

These five architecting failures—only a handful of the possible ones—make the case for a more holistic approach to transformation. Yet, we see little evidence of enterprises doing this effectively. Perhaps this is because it is difficult to understand an enterprise as a whole, and to develop change strategies accordingly. Maybe that's why traditional approaches have focused so heavily on information technology, with insufficient attention to other dimensions, such as process, culture, and organization. Other useful yet limited approaches have placed a strong emphasis on process but failed to consider other important enterprise aspects. More recently, some business model–focused approaches have targeted strategic issues, but in our view, they still do not provide everything needed for a truly holistic enterprise transformation. Let's take a closer look at these five failures, remembering, of course, that there are numerous others.

Failure 1: When in Doubt, Reorganize

One very common potential failure stems from the "when in doubt, reorganize" approach. It seems as if almost every enterprise has tried this at one time or another. In our studies, we observe that the most frequent changes to the architecture relate to the organizational structure. Enterprises often, shortsightedly, turn to reorganizing as the solution to whatever they face. But what if the real problem lies, say, with the incentive structure rather than with the reporting structure? While reorganizations can sometimes be necessary, they can be counterproductive when undertaken in isolation from, or without adequate consideration of, other enterprise elements. Rarely does reorganization alone achieve the desired results or a genuine enterprise transformation. More often than not, reorganizations, even when they are necessary and beneficial, are highly disruptive to internal stakeholders. This is particularly true if the new organization is not aligned with the business processes or the information architecture, for example, or doesn't quite fit the legacy culture.

Consider the case of a large equipment manufacturer that decided to centralize its customer support across all divisions with the objective of better servicing customer needs. They announced the new organization without the corresponding mechanisms in place for coordinating with the engineering and technical sales groups in the individual divisions. No provisions had been made for the new processes and IT infrastructure required, resulting in mass chaos and customer dissatisfaction for an extended period of time.

Failure 2: Forgetting Stakeholders

The next type of failure is more common than you might expect: forgetting stakeholders. Enterprises exist to deliver value to stakeholders, but it is surprisingly easy to forget to elicit genuine stakeholder needs and desires during transformation efforts. Listening to the voice of the customer is basic leadership practice, but this alone is not enough. A change in the enterprise affects many stakeholders, such as employees, shareholders, business partners, suppliers, and others. Often the enterprise simply forgets to involve all relevant stakeholders in a transformation initiative. Enterprises also sometimes simply assume they know what stakeholders want, thinking it unnecessary to consult with them. They may also think they know what is best for their stakeholders, even if the stakeholders themselves don't know. Making big changes without "socializing" ideas for change is bound to cause problems later.

The Netflix decision in 2011 to split its DVD-by-mail service from its online streaming service into a separate business called Quikster is a great example of forgetting the stakeholders. It was not just that the decision was poorly timed to follow a significant, and highly unpopular, price increase for members. The company, failing to perform adequate stakeholder analysis, was blindsided by the level of pushback from its customer base. A second stakeholder group, the shareholders, was impacted as well when the stock price fell. Less than a month later, Netflix wisely reversed the decision on Quikster.[5] We have to think that this caused internal confusion as the workforce began to implement the new business practice, then had to revert to the former one.

Failure 3: It Is All about Technology

The next failure type is thinking it is all about technology. Technology, of course, is critically important to almost every modern enterprise. It is a problem, though, when an enterprise sees technology as a "silver bullet" in transforming the enterprise. We have often seen this in the aerospace industry, for example, where there has long been a strong technology paradigm sometimes referred to as "higher, faster, farther," denoting competition based on product performance alone.

We also see this type of failure in technology start-ups. They focus so much on creating the product technology that they are unable to transform because the enterprise was not designed to account for other critical aspects. They may do well for a while, but once competitors enter their market, the technology offering alone is no longer enough to sustain the firm.

A similar failure occurs when enterprises make the mistake of treating the implementation of a new technology as the transformation initiative. Take hospitals, for example. We have seen many cases where everything is designed around the latest technology, but all kinds of issues arise if no one has considered what other things need to change. It does not take long to find out that the introduction of new technology can alter how people work, so it will be problematic if processes and staff responsibilities have not been adjusted accordingly, and if services to maintain the necessary infrastructure are not part of the rearchitected hospital unit.

Failure 4: Silo Effects

Another type of architecting failure is rooted in so-called silo effects. Silos are where groups or functions in the enterprise operate in isolation, and information fails to flow between them. Silos within an enterprise lead to failure that can occur in two ways. One is by optimizing a particular part of the organization, say engineering or manufacturing, at the expense of the rest of the enterprise. The other is by optimizing a specific enterprise element such as processes, organization, or infrastructure in isolation from the others, creating a "silo mentality." This presents significant problems when one silo makes improvements to an area they are responsible for, often with the best intentions, but without considering the impact on other parts of the enterprise.

Many times, the performance measures and incentive systems are to blame. When leaders are measured only on their specific responsibilities, without considering the whole enterprise, suboptimal choices and behaviors are more likely.

In other instances, we have found that there is a simple lack of understanding of the impacts across boundaries. When one particular element of the enterprise (e.g., process, organization, or infrastructure) is optimized in isolation from the others, the outcome is that one part works really well, but may negatively affect other parts of the enterprise.

Failure 5: Information Technology Will Fix Everything

Countless enterprises have made the mistake of thinking information technology (IT) will fix everything—a fifth type of failure. It's not surprising, since much of the enterprise architecture literature focuses heavily on IT, perhaps with minor attention to other elements such as processes and business models. It is not unusual to find cases where the IT department in an enterprise is given the problem statement and charged with solving an enterprise-wide problem. Naturally, these departments tend to employ large complex IT systems as the solution.

While IT systems are a key enabler, failures often occur when an IT solution is implemented without considering strategic imperatives for the larger enterprise. It is really unfair to expect an IT group, no matter how excellent it may be, to take on the transformation in its entirety without participation from stakeholders owning the processes and services supported by the IT department.

An IT-based solution has a clear implementation path, but it is a narrow-minded path unless other aspects and stakeholders of the enterprise are taken into account. Many large organizations, for example, have had difficulties with the implementation of a new enterprise resource planning (ERP) system, because they thought that IT alone would be enough without due consideration of process redesign and stakeholder needs. Many researchers[6] have stressed the importance of alignment of IT with strategy and organizational factors, but even these dimensions are not always given sufficient consideration. Expecting IT alone to fix enterprises is a path to limited success, at best.

The Need for Architecting

Designing a successful transformation and avoiding failures (our five and many others) requires understanding that enterprises are systems.[7] Given that enterprise systems are complex, transforming an enterprise from a current state to a desired future state necessitates a well-specified design or blueprint—what we call an architecture. To succeed, there must be a clear pathway to guide the enterprise in achieving its future design.

Considerable attention has been paid to enterprise transformation over the past two decades. Much is known about effectively managing enterprise change, and many useful frameworks, reference models, and methods have been developed to specify the enterprise architecture at a detailed level. But there's a problem: these existing frameworks, models, and methods focus largely on the activities that happen after simply deciding what the future enterprise architecture will be. That is, the choice of what future architecture the enterprise will transition to is treated as a simple point decision rather than a significant decision analysis problem. The result is that something critically important is largely ignored: how one generates the possibilities for what the future architecture could be, and then methodically evaluates and selects what the architecture should be. The architecture itself is important, but so too is the process of creating the architecture—what we call architecting.

What Is Architecting?

Contemporary architecting is a well-developed field concerned with the conceptual design, planning, and construction of physical structures. Architecting is not new—it goes back millennia, as evidenced by impressive structures that still remain, such as the Egyptian pyramids and Roman aqueducts. Traditionally, architecting has been about the construction of individual structures. In recent decades, architecting has been extended to all types of technological systems (products, technology, information technology, software, etc.) and to enterprises. Regardless of whether the focus is on a technological system or an enterprise system, architecting involves fundamental concepts and constructs.

Consider the case of the building architect, who designs a structure for an envisioned future use. Structures are designed to accommodate, enable, and inspire the behavior of people who will use and interact with them. Designing buildings with both stairs and wheelchair ramps accommodates accessibility for all. Movable wall partitions enable space to be reconfigured dynamically. Open atriums inspire people to interact and engage in unplanned conversations.

Creating an architectural design generates artifacts such as a blueprint illustrating the future structure, and perhaps a built-to-scale model. Metrics are also important considerations for the building architect. For example, the building will need to have physical dimensions that correspond to the footprint of the landscape. It will need to accommodate a certain number of inhabitants or users. Periodicity also comes into play. Is the structure intended to stand forever or does it have a fixed lifespan? Will it be built all at once or in stages over a longer period?

These same aspects—structure, behavior, artifacts, metrics, and periodicity—are the concerns of all architects, including enterprise architects, as we later discuss.

What Does It Mean to Architect an Enterprise?

We have hinted that the enterprise architect does some of the same things as the traditional building architect. There are differences, however. It is sometimes said that enterprise architecting is, in fact, more akin to urban planning. Enterprise architects rarely get to work on a "greenfield," where no existing enterprise operates and few constraints exist. Rather, they design for change to be implemented in a functioning complex system within a living ecosystem. Consider this short parable that uses landscape architecting as a proxy for enterprise architecting to illustrate the point.

An Architecting Parable

You are on the town council and are discussing the empty plot of land that has just been donated to the town. You suggest it would be a great place to create a new public park, given its central location. Everyone else on the council agrees, and you're asked to be in charge of making it happen.

So, what next? Should you draw up a quick sketch and then start planting flowers? Wisely, you decide it might be a good idea to look at some other community parks for ideas. This gets you thinking about how your town's future park could be even better than those in neighboring towns, which might be good for business. Soon, you realize that the project may be beyond your know-how, and you fear that you just don't have enough time to devote to the effort yourself.

You decide to hire a landscape architect to develop several options that you can bring before the town council. First, though, the architect wants to learn more about the current state. You thought an empty lot would make for a "blank slate," but the architect disagrees. She comes over to see your empty plot of land and look at the surrounding environment of roadways, businesses, and foot traffic.

It turns out there's quite a bit to think about. The land has been serving as a place for kids to play soccer, a shortcut for residents to get to a town-center bus stop, and a place for people to walk their dogs. Plus, there's a small, empty building on the property. You assumed it would be torn down. But it turns out it was built more than a hundred years ago, and so it's protected property that has to be incorporated into any future plans.

After the architect takes her tour of the land and environs, she meets with every town council member to ask what they value in a public park. She even asks some citizens. Asking the home and business owners near the property hadn't even occurred to you, but now it seems obvious that it needs to be done. After all, their homes and businesses may be affected by any construction. And while the park may actually draw more people into town and be good for business, some might prefer for things to stay the same.

Fortunately, your architect is smart enough to look into some things you hadn't even considered, such as state conservation regulations, soil conditions, and labor rates for work crews. She also raises some questions no one else had thought about. Who's going to do the landscape upkeep, and how does this figure into the town budget? Will the town take care of maintenance, or will it be outsourced to a landscaping company?

With all the information she's gathered, the architect finally comes up with some preliminary sketches, and the two of you agree that developing detailed blueprints for several of them will be a good way to move forward. She creates several candidate designs for the public park, and you bring them to the next council meeting, figuring the council can vote on which is "best." You're sure that your choice—the one with the sculpture garden—is the best one for the town and others will surely agree.

Surprise! Other members actually favor other options—the one with a dog walk or the one with a sports field—and not the sculpture-garden design that you prefer. They argue over the merits of each.

Your landscape architect expected this, even if you did not. She pulls out the list of what each person originally wanted in the future park, from her earlier discussions. Realizing no concept will make everyone happy, the council decides it will choose based on the top five things everyone agrees are most important. "Everyone" doesn't just mean the council members, but also the home and business owners interviewed. The top five criteria help structure the decision making so that a park that seems best for all concerned can be chosen.

It turns out that the sculpture-garden design comes out on top. It was a tough choice, with the dog-walk design getting some strong consideration.

In the end, the architect comes up with a plan that adds a dog walk into the sculpture-garden architecture, and the final blueprint for the park turns out to be even better suited to everyone's needs and desires. Now you feel confident your transformation of the empty lot will be a success. All that remains is to take it to the mayor for final approval, and then present the plan and how it was chosen at the next town meeting.

You breathe a sigh of relief. What a huge mistake it would have been just to start digging up the turf and planting flowers!

Thinking about This Parable

Now imagine that instead of being a member of the town council you are on the management team of a large corporation, the town mayor is the CEO, and the plot of land is a newly acquired small business. The landscape architect is instead an *enterprise architect*. This time alternative architecture choices relate to integrating the acquisition into an existing business unit, retaining it as a wholly owned subsidiary, or making it a new business unit under the parent corporation. In the end, perhaps the "best" architecture would be to create a new business unit, and to also move some existing pieces of other units into this new unit.

As you think about this parable, you can begin to see the merits of an architectural approach. As with all decision making, jumping to a solution without considering possibilities is not a good tactic, no matter how much urgency there is to implement changes. You may also have concluded that even the simplest transformation initiative turns out to be a complex decision problem, making it potentially very easy to end up with a suboptimal solution. This is why we advocate a holistic approach in architecting the future enterprise.

Architecting Matters

Enterprises most often undertake an enterprise transformation because of an urgent problem, need, or opportunity. In this type of climate, it is easy to see why any of the five failures—or others—might occur. Consider failure types you have observed in your own enterprise, and be watchful for these. It is very easy to repeat history, because the root causes of failures are typically embedded deep in the enterprise culture and in our mental models of how things work.

For a transformation to be successful in the long run, it has to get off to a good start. As Plato said in *The Republic*, "The beginning is the most important part of the work." The biggest limitation of current approaches, in our view, is that enterprise leaders fail to expend sufficient effort in choosing the "right" architecture—the blueprint for the future enterprise.[8] This is precisely why architecting matters.

2 The ARIES Framework

First comes thought; then organization of that thought, into ideas and plans; then transformation of those plans into reality ... the beginning, as you will observe, is in your imagination.

—Napoleon Hill

Our work over the past decade has focused on developing and validating an architecting approach designed specifically for the initial phase of transforming an enterprise. This approach is designed for architecting teams who face starting with a seed idea for enterprise transformation while it is still the "glimmer in the eye" of visionary leaders. The task of moving from new thought to ideas to plans is inherently creative, but that does not mean it is a journey without a roadmap.

Our desire to create such a roadmap has resulted in a new framework accompanied by a collection of supporting constructs and techniques, some new and some tried and true. Our framework, ARIES (Architecting Innovative Enterprise Strategy), is so named to reflect three transformation fundamentals.

Architecting is the act of creating a "blueprint" for the enterprise to follow in order to achieve its desired vision for the future. It involves understanding the current enterprise in the context of the ever-changing environment within which it operates (what we call its ecosystem), creating a holistic vision of the future, generating and evaluating alternatives, and selecting a future architecture to realize the envisioned future. Architecting culminates in an implementation plan that accounts for available resources and a time horizon for completing the transformation.

Innovative means being ahead of the times, or at least forward-looking. An enterprise needs to evolve to stay ahead of changes in its ecosystem that may affect its ability to survive and to thrive. Effective enterprise change involves an informed look-ahead given the best available knowledge and insights regarding the future. Architecting is inherently innovative, and involves a forward-looking perspective.

Enterprise strategy is the overarching strategy of the enterprise. The term *enterprise strategy* was first used in 1979 by Igor Ansoff, widely considered the father of strategic management, followed by Schendel and Hofer, who say that "enterprise strategy attempts to integrate the firm with its broader non-controllable environment."[1] Five years later, Richard Freeman detailed his theory of stakeholders, defining enterprise strategy of a firm as "what it stands for."[2] Foundational ideas such as these shape our view that excellence of an enterprise strategy is the determinant of success in delivering value to stakeholders, while both pulling from and contributing to its own ecosystem.

Why a New Framework?

A question that will likely come to mind is "Why does the world need yet another new enterprise architecting framework, given the plethora of frameworks that already exist?"[3] Our answer to that question lies in the motivations for considering change in the first place. What triggers an enterprise to undertake a transformation? Generally speaking, it is when leadership recognizes the need for innovation in the enterprise strategy and must figure out a way forward. In almost every case, this recognition originates in significant pressures from the changing world surrounding the enterprise. With this comes a strong sense of urgency to take action, and all too often, this compels enterprises to jump almost instantaneously to "the solution," without taking time for thoughtful consideration. This rapid-fire response, more often than not, results in the enterprise going down a less-than-optimal path. Choices are made quickly, but may not be the best ones.

Experience shows that for enterprises about to embark on a transformation, there is never a time when it is more important to weigh change options with care and deliberation. Changing the trajectory of the enterprise is more than a simple design exercise; it demands an extensive, thoughtful approach. This is further complicated by the need to effectively manage "sun-setting" aspects of the existing enterprise, while preparing to launch the new architecture.

Much is known about effective enterprise transformation—theories and case studies are well documented. A substantial body of work has been developed by William Rouse, including works on enterprises as systems, the many facets of enterprise transformation, and transformation case studies.[4] The Tennenbaum Institute at the Georgia Institute of Technology has been a leading academic center for enterprise transformation work since 2004. Excellent work has been ongoing on a global basis for many years in the areas of enterprise transformation and enterprise architecture.

We view our work as harmonized with past and ongoing work, but bringing a new contribution to this field that places an intensive focus on *architecting* as an essential part of complex enterprise transformations. There is a difference between "architecture" and "architecting." Eberhardt Rechtin, considered the founding father of systems architecting, more or less coined this term in the context of the engineering of complex technological systems.[5] He said, "I use 'architecting' so that people focus on the process that an architect does. If I just use 'architecture' it means too many different things, so I invented another word."[6]

In the larger field of enterprise transformation, what has been lacking in our view is a systematic approach for architecting, grounded in research. It is about effectively generating options for the future, evaluating these options, and selecting the future architecture, before enterprise change commences. This activity is what we mean by *architecting the future enterprise*.

What Is the ARIES Framework and When Is It Used?

Our framework draws from the fundamental theory and practice of multiple fields, including strategic management, stakeholder theory, systems architecting, innovation, scenario analysis, decision science, enterprise theory, and systems science. Informed by our work with over one hundred different enterprises of various types, sizes, and levels of complexity and maturity, the ARIES framework is designed to guide the exploratory phase of transformation. ARIES provides a holistic approach to the selection of a new architecture for the future enterprise.

An architecting framework is, of course, not a new idea. In fact, more than a dozen such frameworks are in use. In our view, these frameworks do a good job of guiding the development of a detailed architecture for implementation. Yet, how effective can the many existing formal enterprise architecting frameworks actually be if they support "doing architecting right," but fail to guide the selection of the "right architecture" to begin with?

We believe existing formal frameworks work well in designing a detailed architecture if you choose a good concept for your future enterprise. The fundamental problem is that choosing to go down the enterprise design path without the right *concept architecture* is likely to result in a transformation effort with costly rework, slipped schedules, and underaddressed stakeholder needs. It may, in fact, result in the failure of the enterprise transformation effort as a whole.

Our objective when developing ARIES was not to replace existing frameworks, but to design it to precede and be compatible with the existing formal enterprise architecture frameworks already widely used in industry and government. Its intended use is "upstream" in the transformation lifecycle from where we think existing frameworks are best used (that is, in the detailed design of the architecture). ARIES focuses on effectively exploring the enterprise's possible alternative futures, weighing these options, and methodically selecting the architecture to be the basis for the transformation.

The ARIES framework as portrayed in figure 2.1 consists of (1) the *enterprise element model*, specifying ten unique elements for seeing the whole enterprise; (2) the *architecting process model*, with eight activities; and (3) selected *techniques* and *templates*, some developed through our research and others drawn from existing practice (we introduce these in later chapters).

Seeing the Whole Enterprise

ARIES is grounded in our conviction that an enterprise is a complex system, and accordingly must be treated holistically. It is admittedly quite difficult, from a practical standpoint, to understand an enterprise solely by considering it as a whole. We can examine its constituent parts, but that alone does not help much in understanding the enterprise as a complete system. We can use a single lens—such as a process view or an information technology view—but at the risk of a "monochromatic" perspective that limits seeing the enterprise's inherent richness.

Our research and consultation with enterprises have shown that having a number of unique lenses with which to examine the enterprise makes understanding the whole enterprise tractable. This permits seeing the enterprise from multiple perspectives, each showing something different. We refer to these as *enterprise elements*.

Enterprise elements make it possible to isolate unique areas of focus, and doing this makes it possible to reduce complexity so that the whole enterprise can be examined. Adopting multiple perspectives, which is made possible by these elements, increases the likelihood of uncovering the needs of an enterprise's diverse set of stakeholders so that they are considered in the transformation. Through our work with enterprises of various sizes and types, we have identified ten elements that are fundamental to enterprise architecting. In combination, we refer to these as our *enterprise element model*.

Enterprise Element Model

Our ten-element model is used throughout the architecting process in various ways, which we discuss throughout the book. The first two elements are the *ecosystem* and *stakeholders*. The remaining eight are what we refer to as the *view*

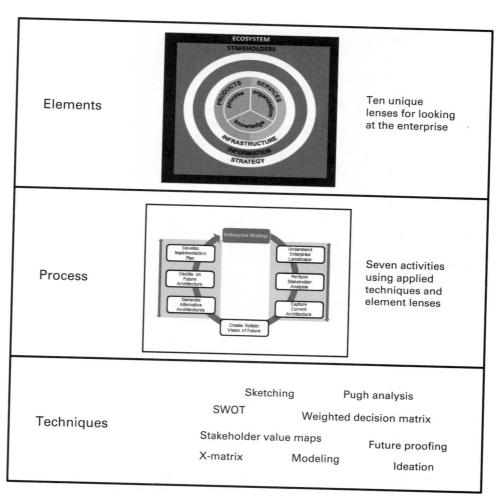

Elements	Ten unique lenses for looking at the enterprise
Process	Seven activities using applied techniques and element lenses
Techniques	

Figure 2.1
ARIES framework

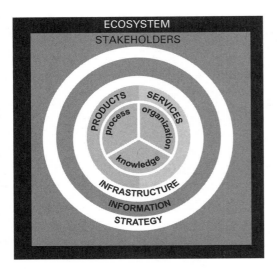

Figure 2.2
ARIES enterprise element model

elements, because they are "lenses" that allow us to look inside the walls of the enterprise from different angles. Figure 2.2 shows the enterprise element model.

The first element, depicted as the black outer rectangle in figure 2.2, is the *ecosystem*. Exogenous to the enterprise, this is the part of the world that is relevant to our particular enterprise. There are likely many other enterprises in our ecosystem, such as competitors, suppliers, and partners. The ecosystem is characterized by the regulatory, political, economic, market, and societal environment in which the enterprise operates in cooperation or competition with other enterprises. We discuss the ecosystem further in chapter 3.

The second element is *stakeholders*. Stakeholders are the people within the ecosystem (e.g., customers, business partners) and within the walls of our own enterprise (e.g., employees). Enterprise stakeholders are individuals and groups who contribute to, benefit from, and/or are affected by the enterprise. Stakeholders may be either exogenous or endogenous to the enterprise, depending on the perspective you take. For example, some enterprises consider suppliers to be an integral part of the enterprise, whereas an enterprise with a different business model might consider suppliers to be external. In chapter 4, we discuss stakeholders in greater detail, including how different enterprises perceive and engage with their stakeholders.

As noted, we call the remaining eight elements collectively the view elements. These enable us to look within the enterprise. The first of the view elements is the *strategy element*, which includes aspects of the enterprise such as the business model, business strategies, and core values of the enterprise, along with performance management objectives and enterprise metrics.

Closely coupled with strategy is the *information element*, shown as the next ring in figure 2.2. Information is what flows throughout the enterprise and enables it to perform its mission and operate effectively. Information relates to all aspects of the enterprise, from administrative and financial data, to products and services data, to personnel data. At the highest level, it encompasses all strategic and operational information about the enterprise.

In our element model, the strategy and information elements surround the *infrastructure element*, which refers to the information technology and enterprise systems, communication technology, and physical facilities that support the enterprise. Infrastructure enables the enterprise to effectively and efficiently accomplish its mission.

The next two elements are a coupled set; both will be present in many enterprises. The *products element* includes things that the enterprise acquires, markets, develops, manufactures, and/or distributes to stakeholders. The *services element* includes the offerings derived from enterprise knowledge, skills, and competencies that deliver value to stakeholders. Services can include support for the enterprise products.

The remaining three elements are tightly interrelated and are at the core of the enterprise, as depicted at the center of figure 2.2. The *process element* includes leadership, lifecycle, and enabling processes by which the enterprise creates value for its stakeholders. The *organization element* encompasses the organizational structure, including groupings and hierarchies, as well as the underlying social network and culture of the enterprise. Finally, the *knowledge element* comprises the competencies, explicit and tacit knowledge, and intellectual property resident in the enterprise.

These ten elements, as a collection, form the enterprise element model, designed to guide architects to think holistically. The combination of elements brings one closer to seeing the whole enterprise, something not possible by a singular focus—for example, only on the enabling infrastructure or only on processes.

Why These Ten Elements?

One of the questions that may come to mind is "Why these ten elements?" The answer is that the ten elements have emerged as fundamental through our years of work. While other elements have been suggested and tested, ultimately we decided that they are not fundamental but rather crosscutting and part of multiple fundamental elements. For instance, we considered a separate incentive element, but found that incentives cross the strategy and organization elements. Formal incentives are defined and executed as part of strategy; in an organization, the underlying social network may create emergent and informal incentives. A culture-related element has also been suggested, but we place culture within the organization element, embodied in individuals in the workforce, as shaped by their values and experiences.

The suggestion to have a separate financial element comes up frequently, but we believe that financial perspectives are part of many of the other elements. For example, financial targets and objectives are an integral part of strategy. Products and services create opportunities and limitations for an enterprise's financial health. In most mature enterprises, financial management is a core business process. Taking a separate finance view would run counter to the holistic perspective, because finance does not exist on its own in the enterprise.

The ten elements evolved in the course of our work with many types of enterprises over the last decade. Some of these elements were not always considered as fundamental but as part of other elements, and it is worth mentioning why they rose to the fundamental level. For instance, the knowledge element was originally subsumed under organization and what we previously called the information technology element (which has been the traditional focus of enterprise architecting). We then broke apart information (including information technology) and knowledge. More recently, we realized that information technology was only one of several important enabling infrastructures, and so we created an infrastructure element to capture this broader scope. We originally considered services to be supporting products, but we have since made them unique elements. As we began to work with enterprises that were not focused on physical products, such as those in the healthcare and financial sectors, we began to understand the need for a service element separate from product.

The ten enterprise elements flow from our empirical research to date. Of course, we recognize the dynamic nature of research, which may cause the element set to change. These ten have, though, proven to work by providing the fundamental elements necessary for a whole-enterprise perspective. Table 2.1 provides a basic description of each of the ten elements. While not all may be prominent in every enterprise, nor essential to every transformation initiative, neglecting to consider any of them may result in failure to uncover complex systems issues.

All ten elements are linked inextricably, though from enterprise to enterprise some tend to be more important than others. The relative importance of elements in an early start-up enterprise, for example, is almost always different from their significance in a long-established firm. The relative importance of the

Table 2.1

Ten elements of the enterprise

Element	Description
Ecosystem	The external regulatory, political, economic, market, and societal environment in which the enterprise operates and competes/cooperates with other enterprises
Stakeholders	Individuals and groups who contribute to, benefit from, and/or are affected by the enterprise
Strategy	The strategic vision along with the associated business model and key strategic thrusts, goals, and performance management system
Information	Information the enterprise requires to perform its mission and operate effectively in accordance with its strategy
Infrastructure	Enterprise enabling systems and information technology, communication technology, and physical facilities that enable enterprise performance
Products	Products the enterprise acquires, markets, develops, manufactures, and/or distributes to stakeholders
Services	Offerings derived from enterprise knowledge, expertise, and competencies that deliver value to stakeholders, including support of products
Process	Key leadership, lifecycle, and enabling processes by which the enterprise carries out its mission and creates value for its stakeholders
Organization	Culture, organizational structure, and underlying social network of the enterprise
Knowledge	Competencies, expertise, explicit and tacit knowledge, and intellectual property resident in and generated by the enterprise

elements in any particular enterprise also depends, to a large extent, on the enterprise's strategic objectives.

Entanglement of Elements

Some elements directly influence or drive other elements. Some interact with one another and drive enterprise performance in both directions. Unless important interactions across the elements are identified, the dynamics of the enterprise will not be uncovered. Any relationships, dependencies, and tensions that exist across the elements must be considered. For this reason, we like to refer to the elements as *entangled*. This becomes evident in how differently they behave if you look at only one element in isolation, as opposed to considering multiple elements together. Take, for example, strategy. It is a key driver of the architecture of the process, organization, knowledge, and information elements. The information architecture, though, is not only driven by strategy, but also by process, organization, products, and services. They are entangled. Infrastructure plays an enabling role for knowledge, since information technology is so central to facilitating the availability, accessibility, and synthesis of knowledge. Entanglement of the elements differs from enterprise to enterprise. There are differences in how important one interaction may be compared with another, and there is directionality to the interactions. For instance, the direction and influence of an element may be in only one direction, or they may be bidirectional.

To fully understand the elements and the entanglements among them, an in-depth examination of all elements, as they manifest in your particular enterprise, is essential. Because elements are the core of the holistic approach to architecting the enterprise, we believe elements must be analyzed collectively rather than just individually. It's difficult to see the whole enterprise without examining it through the parts (elements), but it's important to recognize that the simple sum of these elements does not equal the whole enterprise.

An Illustrative Case

To illustrate the central role of elements in the ARIES approach, let's consider an enterprise that will likely be familiar to most readers: Starbucks Corporation. Our brief glimpse here, drawn from the literature, shows that one can understand much about an entire enterprise without complete knowledge of every detail.

The key characteristics of the Starbucks strategy include things that you may notice when you go into your local store. Its strategy is to educate customers about quality coffee and to create a retail environment that makes it a pleasurable experience to consume that coffee. Further, Starbucks has a strategy based on procuring quality ingredients for its products, and it continues to expand its offerings by introducing new drinks and food. The product portfolio extends beyond beverages and food to sales of coffee-related products such as mugs, gift packages, and many other things lining the shelves. A key aspect of the strategy is to maintain consistency in products and services across all stores, both in terms of menu items and in the consistent high quality of the coffee products and services delivered by baristas who receive rigorous training.

The Starbucks strategy element has an important relationship with the product and service elements. The enterprise lives and dies by the quality of its products and services. The strategy is linked very closely to both the process and organization elements. Highly standardized processes are used to ensure quality and consistency in products and services. Pride in quality can be linked to the fact that all employees are considered valued partners in the business.

What matters most to Starbucks in its ecosystem? For one thing, the enterprise is concerned about fair trade policies, being environmentally friendly, and adhering to health and environmental standards wherever it has locations. The company wants to engage the local community and values how it cares for employees and customers. These characteristics link the policy aspects of its ecosystem closely to the process element, because processes are driven by policy (for example, fair trade). Health standards, for instance, create a very strong interrelationship between the policy and product elements. Policy and strategy share a close interrelationship as well.

The process element at Starbucks is a strong one. Its well-formalized standard processes provide consistency in product and customer experience; high-quality, long-term relationships with suppliers; smart selection of store locations; consistent, standardized orientation for new employees offered by more experienced employees; and continuous feedback from employees and customers. This creates several important element relationships. Process is closely linked to policy with respect to purchasing beans from suppliers, as well as in the training of employees and the benefits they receive. Process and the organization elements interact in terms of the enterprise's specific organizational strategies for procurement, store organization, training, and human resources.

For the organization element, several key characteristics stand out. One is that everything is corporate owned (except outside of the United States). Starbucks sources its raw materials internationally but processes them centrally. There is an infrastructure for disseminating knowledge. Organization, therefore, has an important relationship with the knowledge, process, and product elements. The organization is structured to provide consistent product quality.

The key characteristic of the knowledge element at Starbucks is the understanding of the products—from quality of beans to roasting. Knowledge resides in all its employees, and training excellence ensures consistent knowledge across the enterprise. Customer feedback and market research inform corporate knowledge. By understanding where Starbucks's products come from, the enterprise learns best practices from others and engages suppliers in its knowledge base. Knowledge interacts strongly with strategy, since knowledge is the foundation of strategy. Both the product and the services element are closely linked to knowledge.

Starbucks has an enabling infrastructure characterized by high standardization, with selective replication throughout the enterprise. Information technology is particularly important within the enabling-infrastructure element. The process and knowledge elements are closely related, since the enabling process and IT infrastructure make it possible for knowledge to be amassed and analyzed. Strategy also interacts strongly with the enabling infrastructure—for example, in its approach to the design of stores.

Finally, we have the Starbucks product and service elements. The product element is characterized by quality and reproducibility, scalability in the range of product offerings, the ability of Starbucks to customize its products, sustainability, and the firm's collaborations with several other enterprises, including United Airlines, Aramark, Pepsico, and Marriott. The product element has important relationships with strategy, processes, and perhaps most clearly with services. The Starbucks service element is characterized by its customer experience, as well as by demonstrating high corporate values, being scalable, and maintaining a business that is sustainable and socially responsible. Service is closely related to strategy, because services are the execution of the strategy; to processes, through which services are executed in support of the strategy; and, of course, to products, with which Starbucks services are holistically integrated.

Now, imagine the outcome if a team working on an enterprise architecting project for Starbucks thought only about information technology or only about the enterprise's processes in isolation. Failure to consider all relevant elements will surely lead to a suboptimal outcome—great performance in one aspect of the enterprise, but at the expense of others.

Now that we have described the enterprise element model and illustrated it with an example, we turn to the architecting process for guiding the architecting team in its activities.

ARIES Process Model

The ARIES process model defines seven activities to be performed in sequence, as shown in figure 2.3. Moving clockwise from top right to top left, the sequence begins with understanding the enterprise landscape, performing stakeholder analysis, and capturing the current architecture. It proceeds with creating a holistic vision of the future and generating alternative architectures. Deciding on the future architecture comes next, followed by developing the implementation plan for the future architecture. Once an implementation plan is completed, the implementation design can commence.

Let us now take a brief look at the seven activities, each of which we present in more detail in subsequent chapters.

Activity 1: Understand the Enterprise Landscape
The first activity is to understand the landscape in which the enterprise sits. The landscape consists of both an internal and an external part. The external part (the *ecosystem*) is that part of the world relevant to our enterprise. Within this ecosystem are other interrelated enterprises (e.g., partners, suppliers, competitors, government agencies). There are context factors that characterize the external environment, such as market factors, economic factors, and regulatory factors. The strategic imperatives and motivations for change are often rooted

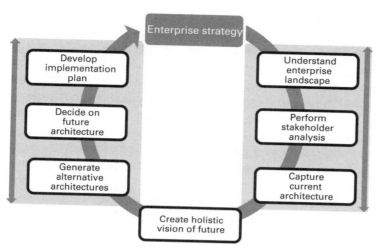

Figure 2.3
ARIES process model

in changes in the ecosystem, so the architecting team will want to examine these carefully. The internal landscape provides both the diversity and the stability for the enterprise's operation in its ecosystem. Typically, the ideology and core values will be constants, but the question of whether they need to be adjusted should be posed in a transformation. High-level strategic transformation goals and objectives, perhaps including changes in the business model, are a focus at this stage; these determine the scope and boundaries for the transformation initiative. During this activity, the architecting team will begin to think about the implementation plan, capturing any early insights regarding enablers and barriers to transformation. This is the time to determine enterprise capabilities (e.g., scalability, adaptability, agility) that presently exist, and those needed in the future. We discuss the *enterprise landscape* in more detail in chapter 3.

Activity 2: Perform Stakeholder Analysis

With an understanding of the enterprise landscape, the next activity in the architecting process is to examine what the stakeholders value. In stakeholder analysis, key internal stakeholders are engaged, and sometimes it is both useful and necessary to involve relevant exogenous stakeholders in some way. These exogenous stakeholders are those outside the enterprise boundary, yet who have an interest or "stake" in the enterprise transformation. Through the stakeholder analysis, an understanding of all the individuals and groups that influence or are influenced by the enterprise is developed. We advocate a value-focused approach to uncover gaps between the value stakeholders desire and the value actually delivered, as well as gaps between current value delivery and anticipated future needs. In this step, the architecting team captures early insights of how the future architecture will be validated in regard to existing and future stakeholder needs. Stakeholder analysis is an essential activity in architecting, and there are a number of techniques that facilitate doing this effectively, as we discuss in chapter 4.

Activity 3: Capture the Current Architecture

Following stakeholder analysis, attention shifts to how the enterprise is currently structured and how it operates. This activity typically involves significant effort to capture the architecture of the current enterprise (*as-is architecture*). Some enterprises may already have a documented formal architecture. If so, some work is still required to determine if the documented as-is architecture aligns with current reality (that is rarely the case, because the enterprise evolves), and noting any deviations. In this activity, the architecting team investigates and documents the current state using the enterprise element model as a guide for a comprehensive inquiry. This necessitates delving deeper into element interactions, current capabilities of the enterprise, and the degree of alignment of strategic objectives, core processes, stakeholder values, and enterprise performance measures. A basic assessment using SWOT (strengths-weaknesses-opportunities-threats) or similar techniques is used to gain insight. We discuss this activity further in chapter 5.

Activity 4: Create a Holistic Vision of the Future

Once the current enterprise is captured, the next step is to create a holistic vision of the future enterprise. A time horizon for transformation is determined based on leadership guidance and on any driving factors (e.g., the date when a new policy regulation takes effect). The context factors (identified in activity 1) are important in creating the envisioned future. The architecting team needs to understand, to the extent possible, whether there are new factors and influences the enterprise may encounter given the time horizon for transformation. Similarly, it's important to anticipate possible shifts in stakeholder value that could occur as transformation progresses. The elements and element interactions are employed here as lenses to elaborate the vision and gain insight into which elements will be critical to realizing the vision. In conjunction with formulating the vision, the architecting team will decide on an architecting evaluation method for selecting a preferred future architecture from among a set of alternatives. Enterprise capabilities often play an important role in this evaluation. We discuss this activity further in chapter 6.

Activity 5: Generate Alternative Architectures

Given an understanding of the present and anticipated future ecosystem and stakeholders, the current architecture, and the holistic vision, the team turns to the task of generating alternative architectures. As we discuss in chapter 7, concepts first need to be explored to open up the possibilities. Generating concepts is probably the most challenging work for an architecting team, relying heavily on creativity. The concept generation helps the team "think outside the box" and build knowledge of what might work. Ideas and knowledge from the first round are combined and refined, resulting in alternative architectures with more detail than the concepts. The ten enterprise elements foster holistic thinking, and we recommend an order for thinking about the elements. Using an *element anatomy,* as we discuss in chapter 5, alternative architectures are elaborated in sufficient detail to permit a formal evaluation. Where in the first round we set aside viability, cost, and risk, we now bring these into the picture, along with thinking about the implementability. Typically, a team will develop three to five viable alternative architectures. Chapter 7 discusses this activity.

Activity 6: Decide on the Future Architecture

Once the set of viable alternative architectures is agreed on (those the team believes could be effective for achieving the envisioned future), decision makers beyond the architecting team may become involved. Depending on the selected evaluation method, the evaluators may be limited to the team or may extend to other stakeholders in the enterprise, and possibly exogenous stakeholders such as customers or suppliers. Applying the chosen evaluation method and selection criteria (we discuss the development of these in chapter 6), the architectures are scored using the criteria and rated with other selected indices (e.g., risk, implementability). The holistic vision makes it possible to discern how well suited each alternative is for one or more envisioned future contexts. The evaluation captures the insights and assumptions of the team members. Closer examination of the architectures may lead to small refinements of these. In an ideal situation, the choice of architecture falls out of the evaluation. In practice, we observe that this is often not the case. We frequently find that teams do not simply select the architecture that garners the highest evaluation but rather, after a round of evaluation, discover positive and negative features in all the alternatives. Based on this, the team derives a "hybrid" architecture by combining positive features from two or more alternatives. Preliminary approval from leadership is desired at this step, to ensure buy-in and support prior to developing the to-be architecture in more detail. We discuss evaluation and selection in chapter 8.

Activity 7: Develop the Implementation Plan

At this point, further detail is needed to build an elaborated description of the selected architecture. The elements, again considered in sequence, result in a detailed anatomy for each element and a description of the interactions between elements. Capturing details of the element interactions is particularly important to achieving a holistic result. Gaps between the as-is and to-be architectures are identified. It is important to ensure the to-be architecture is traceable to capabilities captured earlier. An implementation plan is then developed, including resources, timelines, and roles and responsibilities. It includes a communication strategy for informing and engaging stakeholders as the effort goes forward. This plan is largely about the "what." It is the basis of subsequent detailed implementation planning by experts in the respective enterprise functions. The implementation planning activity is the subject of chapter 9.

Throughout each of the seven activities the architecting team selectively uses a variety of techniques. In the chapters that follow, we take a closer look at all the ARIES architecting activities, and introduce some of the possible techniques that can be used. We illustrate the activities with examples drawn from our studies of real-world enterprises. We begin in the next chapter with the first activity, understanding the enterprise landscape.

3 Understanding the Enterprise Landscape

We know from science that nothing in the universe exists as an isolated or independent entity.

—Margaret J. Wheatley

Enterprises have both an internal and an external landscape. Understanding the enterprise landscape is the first activity in the ARIES process. What exactly do we mean by *enterprise landscape,* and what does a landscape have to do with transformation? A good way to explain this is through a simple analogy.

Imagine the home you live in as an enterprise. Your home includes not only the housing structure itself, but also the property you own on which your house sits. This property can be thought of as the *internal landscape.* It is part of your environment—the part that is under your direct control for the most part. Between the internal and external landscape, there is a defined boundary that divides the property you own and the land owned by others. This dividing boundary might be easy to determine—for instance, when there is a physical boundary such as a fence surrounding your personal property. Even if it is not visible, the boundary still exists. For the most part, you have control over what is inside your property line, subject to special zoning laws or regulations.

Beyond the boundary of your property is the town in which you live, the *external landscape.* This larger environment that surrounds your property is an *ecosystem* that is constantly evolving. Buildings may come and go, new roadways may be created, and the town government periodically sets new rules. You may be able to influence but not control things within this ever-changing external landscape.

As with your home, an enterprise has an inner and outer landscape—that is, both within and outside the enterprise boundary. The outside landscape, or external world that surrounds the enterprise, is the larger ecosystem in which the enterprise exists. We believe it is absolutely essential to think proactively about the future enterprise in the context of its changing ecosystem. Transformation is triggered largely by the need to respond to changes and opportunities that result from a dynamic world. It is essential to understand the ecosystem, as well as the fundamental characteristics that make our enterprise unique and successful within this ecosystem.

The internal landscape is the topography that is the backdrop for transformation. It includes ideology and core values, and with an eye to the future, the strategic imperatives that guide future directions of the enterprise. Deep understanding of the inner landscape is critical to developing an informed perspective from which transformation must flow.

For any given transformation, the landscape is unique. The architecting team needs a shared understanding of where the internal landscape ends and the external landscape begins. It is, in reality, a porous boundary. Nonetheless, the team needs to agree on what will be considered inside the internal landscape, and what will be considered part of the larger ecosystem.

Identifying Scope and Boundaries

The architecting team must understand the boundaries of the enterprise (defining the specific footprint within the larger enterprise), relevant to the transformation.[1] This is not as simple as it sounds. An enterprise is defined contextually. Boundaries come into play with respect to the architecting objectives. We might be architecting a program enterprise—for instance, an automaker's program enterprise might be the development and manufacture of a specific family of automobiles. It might be a multiprogram enterprise that includes all the cars it produces, crossing multiple families of vehicles. Or it may be the global enterprise, including everything in the corporation that adds to the value exchange across the globe.

A start-up company with ten partners is an enterprise, just as is a global financial services company with 50,000 employees. Within that larger global enterprise, a division that handles one aspect of the business, say, credit services, may be considered that segment of the larger enterprise that is the focus of the architecting effort. Bounding is about deciding which parts of the enterprise and the ecosystem are in or out of the transformation "territory."

Defining the scope is about determining the specific focus given the desired enterprise change. The scope of the transformation might be a specific business opportunity or how to extend the workforce (e.g., via outsourcing, hiring, or an acquisition). Specific objectives, ecosystem factors, and constraints may limit the extent of the possible transformation. Scoping requires making a determination about the physical, logical, and operational aspects that will or will not be candidates for change. For example, moving or consolidating facilities may not be deemed an option, but the allocation of workers to facilities could be within scope. Further, the enterprise must determine which stakeholder groups are relevant given the scope, and which parts of the organization are directly involved or indirectly impacted. Their particular relevance to the architecting effort is part of the stakeholder analysis, which we discuss in chapter 4. As with stakeholders, aspects of the enterprise's overall infrastructure, as well as particular business strategies and policies, may be particularly relevant. This will become clear in chapter 5 as the multiple elements are employed to capture the as-is enterprise architecture.

Once the boundaries and scope for the transformation are defined, the architecting team can investigate the enterprise landscape in more detail. The most important dimensions of each major ecosystem factor (e.g., economic, market, regulatory, etc.) will need to be investigated and monitored. The team will want to explore the recent history of the enterprise to look for trends in gradual shifts, or disruptive shifts, as related to the dimensions for each factor. All of these things need to be given thought before moving forward.

Looking outward, it is essential to recognize existing gaps and opportunities, and to identify emerging needs, threats, and opportunities in the changing world around the enterprise. This knowledge can help clarify what is essential for achieving the targeted transformation, and perhaps also what is urgent within the selected time horizon given the forces in the surrounding environment. This is the time to take stock of current enterprise capabilities, and those the enterprise needs to have in the future. Understanding strategic imperatives, enterprise capabilities, and the ecosystem, is the foundation for the thinking that will drive the ideas, strategies, and decisions.

Enterprise Ecosystem (External Landscape)

The task now facing the architecting team is to understand its ecosystem, the external landscape in which the enterprise sits. It is all too easy to make assumptions about this world around our enterprise, and to believe we already understand it. These are some of the most dangerous assumptions that can be made in transformation projects because the likelihood of making bad decisions is high if the architecting team fails to adequately understand the value-driving factors in the ecosystem. By value-driving we mean factors that influence stakeholder perception of the enterprise's products and services. For example, an economic downturn will likely make high-end luxury products less attractive to customers. At the same time, it's important to think about how these will shift in the future. If there appears to be an economic recovery on the horizon, the enterprise may want to shift some of its product research toward its high-end product line.

The ecosystem term is borrowed from biology and ecology. An *enterprise ecosystem*, the world in which the enterprise exists, consists of an interconnected collection of other enterprises, stakeholders, and resources with a direct or secondary impact on the value (received and/or delivered) of our enterprise. The economic, political, regulatory, and market conditions determine the climate. Constituents of the enterprise may include partners, competitors, suppliers, government agencies, and other entities. There are dependencies and interrelationships among the ecosystem constituents. The ability to thrive could well depend on the existence and health of other enterprise constituents, and on how the ecosystem evolves.

As we examine the enterprise ecosystem further, we can begin to identify areas of uncertainty. We may believe there is uncertainty related to economic policies following a change in political administrations. We could be uncertain whether a particular new technology will be available in time for its use in our new product line. We may be unsure whether our supplier base will be adequate if we double our business. The architecting team will want to identify the most important ecosystem factors and related uncertainties that the enterprise faces now, and those that it may be likely to face in the future.

Uncertainty and Influencing Factors in the Ecosystem

Ecosystem factors are the exogenous (to our enterprise) factors that are within the bounds of our ecosystem. They bring unique influences and uncertainties into play. These factors shift over time in response to a changing world, and these shifts can and often do affect the enterprise in both positive and negative ways. Ecosystem factors may include economic, political, environmental, resource, technology, and market-related factors. Our studies of enterprises show the trigger for transformation often stems from a shift (anticipated or actual) in one or more of these factors.[2]

Table 3.1 describes seven important ecosystem factors, with examples of triggers that may cause a shift that impacts the enterprise in some way, thus driving the need to transform. The architecting team will want to consider which of these seven, as well as other ecosystem factors, are important.

Take the case where U.S. enterprises in the 1970s became able to trade with China, having been locked out of that huge market for decades. In many cases, enterprises were not immediately ready to adapt to such a change in the ecosystem to take advantage of this new opportunity. Sometimes circumstances like this may seem to come out of nowhere, causing an unanticipated sudden

Table 3.1

Enterprise ecosystem factors

Ecosystem factor	Examples of shifts that may trigger enterprise transformation
Politics	• A new government comes to power, impacting investor behavior. • An anticipated election cycle affects leadership change.
Regulation	• New policies restrict countries where the enterprise may operate. • Introduction of more stringent emission standards affects products.
Economy	• A downturn in the global (or national) economy necessitates downsizing. • New venture investment funding dries up for a period.
Market	• A strong, new competitor enters the enterprise's principal market. • The signing of a trade agreement opens the potential for a new market.
Technology	• Disruptive innovation diminishes the attractiveness of the enterprise's products. • A technology innovation shifts the business model to a service-oriented model.
Resource	• Imposition of a mandatory retirement age causes rapid workforce attrition. • Availability of a new material opens new product opportunities.
Environment	• A natural disaster disrupts business in a key region. • Stakeholders begin to clamor for "green" enterprise practices.

shift within the ecosystem. But, if an enterprise is proactive and continuously monitoring its external landscape for trends and indicators, the need to transform can be anticipated in advance. There is a great advantage for enterprises that can anticipate ecosystem factor shifts and be prepared to respond.

What might it mean to be proactive? Imagine a case where a government makes larger-than-usual investments in infrastructure to boost a lagging economy, thus shifting the economic conditions in the ecosystem for many different enterprises. These may include the concrete manufacturer that finds a surge in demand from the construction contractors, the temporary staffing agency that needs to recruit construction workers, and the police force that needs to respond to requests for officers to be at worksites for public safety reasons. For each of these enterprises, the shift in the ecosystem did not have to be a surprise. The policy change was a regular topic of discussion before the government made its investment. A proactive enterprise could anticipate the possibility of this particular future, and begin to investigate the enterprise changes that might be needed to respond. In some cases, the enterprise might even be able to influence the actual outcome through lobbying or similar activity.

Technological innovations often force an enterprise to shift its business model altogether. That is what happened with IBM, as it evolved from its dominant focus on selling mainframes to global services. The success of this major enterprise transformation is a well-known story,[3] but not every enterprise facing similar circumstances has been as successful.

Disruptive innovations can create shifts that basically eliminate whole product categories. Portable compact disc players, for example, were made obsolete by the iPod.[4] Significant shifts in the enterprise ecosystem demand that the enterprise either be robust or resilient to the change, or that it take timely action to adapt to the shift. Enterprise capabilities can be designed into the architecture to enable the enterprise to respond to anticipated ecosystem shifts, as well as survive significant and unanticipated disruptions.

The explicit identification of ecosystem factors is an important task for the architecting team as it seeks to understand its enterprise ecosystem. For a large enterprise, there are many dimensions for each factor. While all are important to the enterprise as a whole, there will be dominant factors the team will need to monitor and consider in a transformation effort. Once these factors and the relevant dimension(s) are identified, specific details can be examined, including the triggers that may cause a shift.

Consider the regulatory ecosystem factor. This factor covers a lot of territory, so it is important for the architecting team to identify what is specifically relevant to the transformation activity. For example, many equipment manufacturing companies closely track policy for emission standards. In 2004 the US Environmental Protection Agency (EPA) announced the Tier 4 emissions standard to be phased into engines by 2015. The change in the emission standard was a major driver for transformation within the product development and support divisions in these enterprises, since the policy for emission standards is a key factor for these divisions. In contrast, a division within that enterprise that provides financial services to customers likely monitors the ecosystem for shifts in taxation and interest rate regulations as its most important regulatory factor.

This architecting activity could, in theory, go on forever since the world is constantly changing. The investigation of the landscape—both internal and external—is the necessary first task. The architecting team gains important knowledge as a result but, of course, this knowledge is incomplete. As a result, the architecting team will want to keep watch, throughout the architecting project, for any significant shifts within the internal and external landscape that could either put the transformation at risk or create opportunities.

Internal Landscape

Understanding the internal landscape by looking inside the enterprise takes effort. One cannot assume this internal landscape is known, and that effort is not necessary. Rather, it is always important to investigate the internal landscape to ensure all leveraging factors and problem areas are identified. The architecting team needs a shared picture of this internal landscape.

It involves looking at the foundational elements, ideology, and core values. Strategic imperatives, necessary for the enterprise's success into the future, need to be identified and validated with the leadership. There needs to be an inventory of current capabilities, and a sense for where new capabilities will be helpful in the future. The architecting team needs a clear understanding of the motivations for change in order to later formulate future strategies. The challenge for the team is to discern which dominant driving factors require focus in the scope of a given transformation activity. The team cannot possibly take into account every aspect. Scope and boundary decisions are necessary to make the transformation activity tractable for the architecting team.

Identity of the Enterprise

Every enterprise has its own unique identity, and having this identity has multiple dimensions. Whole Foods Market promotes health and caring for the environment and communities, and focuses on selling the highest-quality natural and organic products with local product and produce sourcing. Trader Joe's dedicates itself to providing value to its customers through great food, a unique house brand, great prices, and neighborhood involvement. Costco, a membership warehouse club, focuses on bringing its members the best possible prices on brand-name merchandise. Understanding the various dimensions of the enterprise's identity is a prerequisite for an architecting team's work. In the case where the team members come from outside the enterprise or are new to the enterprise, this is especially important since it will not be implicitly understood. Whether consisting of "insiders" or "outsiders," the architecting team will want to agree on what aspects of the identity must be protected.

As the project gets underway, the architecting team needs to understand the motivations for change (who? what? why?) and, accordingly, the strategic imperatives. These are essential forward-looking priorities or directions that the enterprise must pursue to achieve its vision. Strategic imperatives may drive the enterprise in new directions, fill gaps, or strengthen weaknesses. That is, they involve change or movement from the current state, while ideology and core values tend to be constants unless there is a major leadership or ownership change.

The architecting team must have a firm grasp of the enterprise ideology and core values. This understanding is best acquired by conversations with enterprise leadership. Insights can also be gained by examining artifacts such as the mission statement, goal-oriented reports, and business measures.

An ideology is the worldview of the enterprise, the enduring system of ideas that is the foundation for the enterprise's highest-level goals, expectations, and cultural beliefs. Generally, the ideology evolves rather slowly over time for the enterprise. Many modern enterprises characterize their ideology as value-centered, with an extended set of principles such as a lean enterprise. Increasingly, many enterprises have sought to shift their ideology to one that focuses on benefits to society at large. These enterprises may describe their enterprise ideology as one with a commitment to being a socially responsible enterprise, green enterprise, or sustainable enterprise.

Having a system of business performance measurements tied to the ideology is a common practice of mature enterprises. Ideology-based goals and measures are likely to cut across many of our ten enterprise elements. It is one thing for an enterprise to say it is socially responsible and another to have demonstrable "evidence."

The *Starbucks Global Responsibility Goals and Progress Report* is a well-crafted example of demonstrated social responsibility, including a scorecard summarizing progress on initiatives.[5] For example, one of the twelve goals in its 2010 report states, "Beginning in December 2010, build all new, company-owned stores to achieve LEED certification." The report then states that progress is on track, giving specific information: "In 2010, we completed the pilot phase for the U.S. Green Building Council's LEED Volume Certification pilot program, with 10 store design and construction projects audited and approved by the USGBC." Each year the company updates the report, demonstrating its progress against plans. The 2011 report observes, "After years of assessment pilots and tests, we are now executing on this new strategy and building 75 percent of all new company-owned stores to be certified under the LEED® green building standard." Goals can be challenging; evidence in the 2012 report includes the following statement: "As the first retail company to take this building approach globally, we've experienced success in some geographic areas and challenges in others. In 2012, we built 69 percent of our new global company-owned stores to achieve LEED, but had difficulty applying LEED in regions where the program is not as established. Going forward, we will explore additional strategies to bring 100% of our stores to a sustainable building standard."

The enterprise architecting team needs to understand the ideology at the start of its work. If nothing else, it will be necessary to show alignment between candidate architectures under consideration and the overall ideology. In some cases, an architecture alternative that is selected may drive an adjustment to, or addition of, a goal or measure. At a minimum, the implementation plan resulting from an enterprise architecting effort needs to describe the relationship of the to-be architecture to relevant enterprise ideology–based mission, goals, and measures. As the team investigates the as-is enterprise, it should keep watch for any gaps in the stated ideology and practice. Imagine, for instance, an enterprise that calls itself green yet uses no recycled products and does not practice recycling.

Guiding Principles

Core values are the constant guiding principles for the enterprise, reflecting its culture. Many enterprises readily share their espoused core values with external stakeholders and encourage their workforce to live by these values. Ideally, the core values guide important decisions and choices.

In transformations, there can be adjustments to bring behavior into alignment with core values. Core values of enduring enterprises tend to remain relatively unchanged over the years, even as the enterprise grows and changes. Deere & Company is a great example. The company was founded in 1837 by John Deere, a blacksmith and inventor, determined to build his business based on integrity, quality, commitment, and innovation. These remain the company's core values to the present day.[6]

Whole Foods Market, a chain of stores selling natural and organic food and other products, refers to its seven core values as "the soul of our company." Underlying each of the seven values are elaborated assertions and beliefs. As an example, one of their core values is satisfying and delighting customers. It has six subelements; one is creating inviting store environments, asserting that Whole Foods designs store environments to *reflect the communities they serve*. We found a nice example of a case where living up to this core value triggered a transformation initiative. After a seven-year-old boy and his parents lobbied for shelf labels in Braille in its Thousand Oaks, California, store, Whole Foods launched a Braille Independence Initiative, selecting its Newtonville, Massachusetts, location as its second installation given the store's proximity to two important schools for the blind.[7] While many enterprises say they have core values, they are meaningless unless the enterprise lives by them.

An enterprise's ideology and its core values should be well aligned; if not, they are certain to be problematic. This alignment or lack of alignment is important information for the architecting team. The core values may serve as evaluation criteria for assessing the "fitness" of candidate architectures (a topic we discuss in chapter 9). They may also suggest aspects of the enterprise that must be retained in the new architecture. Similarly, when misalignment is present in the existing enterprise, it could suggest a need to change core values.

The enterprise architecting team uses the ideology and espoused core values to understand the values of the enterprise. Ideally, this understanding provides the team with a frame within which their selected future architecture must fit. But it can be the case that the team will discover some misalignment between ideology and core values, or a discrepancy between stated ideology and values and their actual acceptance by the workforce. The latter case will prompt a deeper investigation of this gap in investigating the current enterprise (discussed in chapter 5). These discrepancies are likely to trigger ideas and requirements for resolving the gap in the future architecture, and may even require leadership strategies to reshape ideology and core values.

Motivations for Change

A variety of circumstances may motivate the enterprise to make changes. As we have noted, it may be driven by outdated ideology and values, misalignment, or an enterprise culture that fails to embrace its core values. Often, motivations for change come from factors in the ecosystem that threaten the enterprise's ability to survive and thrive in its dynamic world. Motivations may also simply be the desire to be better, or to be prepared for new opportunities given where the world is perceived to be headed. Once motivations are clear, leadership sets strategic imperatives for the enterprise transformation. With those imperatives, the architecting team can begin to formulate specific transformation goals and objectives.

An enterprise may go down the transformation path for any number of reasons. Market opportunities, economic changes, competitive forces, natural evolution of the business, mergers and acquisitions, or the quest for major improvement may necessitate a new architecture. The question to ask is what drives the need for enterprise transformation, which in turn drives the requirement for a change in the enterprise architecture. From there, we can articulate the strategic challenges the enterprise faces that can be addressed by architecture change.

Once these challenges have been articulated, leadership can formulate specific strategic goals and objectives with respect to what the team has discovered. A time horizon for the effort can now be discerned. At this point specific enterprise capabilities that exist, or will be needed, are identified. These capabilities provide important leverage for evolving the enterprise.

Enterprise Capabilities

Enterprise capabilities are the system properties that provide the ability to perform, and to respond to challenges and opportunities in a certain way. Capabilities enable the enterprise to execute a specified course of action when needed. These capabilities are so important because they provide a means to sustain enterprise value delivery over time, given the dynamic world surrounding the enterprise.

The architecting team may find that some enterprise properties exist in the current enterprise and can be leveraged. For example, *workforce scalability* could be implemented by using temporary staff, enabling an enterprise to be responsive to a strategic imperative of downsizing the enterprise. The capabilities may also not yet be present but could be targeted for the future architecture. For instance, replicability of organization and infrastructure (implemented through a franchising approach) might be a targeted capability for a future architecture to support international growth.

Consider an enterprise that has a strategic imperative to expand from a national to an international enterprise. That means that there will be new and possibly unknown factors in its expanded global ecosystem given different markets and policies, for example. *Adaptability* will likely be an important capability, defined as the ability of an enterprise to sustain value delivery by transforming itself to respond to changes in its ecosystem. Adaptability might already exist in our current enterprise, or be a desired characteristic of the to-be enterprise architecture. We do, of course, need to be specific about what aspect of the enterprise architecture provides adaptability. For instance, where adaptability relates to finances, an enterprise may need to change from the use of fixed pricing to a flexible pricing structure, allowing ease of pricing products for different regions with differing economies.

Our research has identified important enterprise capabilities from which modern enterprises benefit. Ten capabilities have surfaced as primary, and an additional six are often in play. There are certainly others, and what capabilities are most important will be both enterprise dependent and a function of the times. For example, during the initial growth of Silicon Valley, competitiveness and scalability were among the most important capabilities a young enterprise needed to thrive. For an enterprise seeking to grow to a franchise, replicability is an essential capability, but replicability may not be wanted or needed in other types of enterprises.

Table 3.2 defines ten enterprise capabilities as we use them; your enterprise may define them differently. What is most important is that the definitions are explicit and accessible to avoid ambiguous decisions.[8] All involved stakeholders need to have shared definitions to avoid misunderstandings.

Table 3.2
Definitions of enterprise capabilities

Adaptability	Ability of an enterprise to sustain value delivery by transforming itself to respond to changes in its ecosystem
Agility	Ability of an enterprise to shift rapidly from one strategy to another to sustain enterprise value delivery
Competitiveness	Ability of an enterprise to deliver products/services that provide value to stakeholders equal to or greater than that of competing enterprises
Evolvability	Capacity of an enterprise to transform by leveraging successful features of the current architecture
Replicability	Ability to reproduce enterprise entities (e.g., products/services, business units) effectively to create or sustain value delivery
Resilience	Ability of an enterprise to cope effectively with changing circumstances and recover from disruptive events
Responsiveness	Ability to respond in a timely and effective way to emergent stakeholder needs, threats, and opportunities
Robustness	Ability to sustain consistent value delivery in spite of changes and perturbations in the enterprise ecosystem
Scalability	Ability to expand or contract the enterprise to meet changing circumstances in order to sustain value delivery
Sustainability	Capacity of an enterprise to endure over time as related to environmental, economic, and/or social dimensions

In addition to the ten enterprise capabilities shown in the table, there are several others we often see used: accountability, autonomy, configurability, effectiveness, modularity, and stability. As time goes by, we see more and more of these types of terms.

Scalability, for example, could be about workforce size or the number of product offerings. An enterprise's scalability might also imply that the underlying business model offers potential for economic growth and that the enterprise itself can grow in size and market share. Adaptability might refer to the ability to operate with multiple business models or the ease in spinning off business units without losing critical operational elements of the enterprise. Robustness characterizes an enterprise that is able to cope well with variations, sometimes unpredictable, in its operating environment, without losing much functionality.

Sometimes a capability may have multiple dimensions, as in the case of sustainability. On the one hand, sustainability refers to the enterprise's ability to maintain market share, processes, functions, diversity, and productivity into the future. On the other, it may imply protecting the environment. Again, it is essential for the architecting team to precisely define what is meant for their particular enterprise.

Starbucks understands *sustainability* in terms of how customers experience its stores, and also incorporates environmental aspects of sustainability as part of its business. Announcing the company's "global store design strategy," one executive said, "We recognize the importance of continuously evolving with our customers' interests, lifestyles and values in order to stay relevant over the long term. Our new design approach will allow customers to feel truly at home when visiting their local store and give them opportunities for discovery at our other locations around the world."[9] Fundamental aspects include ongoing commitment to ethical sourcing and environmental stewardship and community involvement, with the new designs reflecting the character of each store's surrounding neighborhood and helping to reduce environmental impacts.

For any given enterprise, there are likely certain enterprise capabilities that make it possible to transform, particularly if it is adept at using those capabilities when needed. Capabilities can reflect the ease with which a transformation can be realized or achieved. For example, architecting for workforce scalability (e.g., implementing extended staffing through outsourcing or temporary employees such as many retail companies use during peak holiday periods) enables the enterprise to efficiently expand or downsize as business needs change. This is why enterprise capabilities are often criteria used for evaluating the goodness of alternative enterprise architectures (we discuss this in chapter 6).

The internal landscape with strategic imperatives, ideology, core values, and enterprise capabilities will continue to be of central importance in the architecting effort going forward. Knowledge of the external landscape (ecosystem) is more elusive. The nature and dynamics of the ecosystem require continuous monitoring, with a vigilant watch for new transformation triggers, or threats to success. The changing ecosystem is frequently the catalyst for enterprise transformation. The new architecture for the enterprise must, at a minimum, enable it to survive in its ecosystem. A superior architecture will enable the enterprise to thrive.

Given a renewed understanding of the enterprise landscape, the architecting team is now ready to move into the second activity of the ARIES process: *stakeholder analysis*.

Understanding the Enterprise Landscape

Exercises to apply to your own enterprise

- List the major constituents in your enterprise ecosystem (competitors, collaborations, suppliers, etc.).
- Identify the key ecosystem factors for your enterprise and provide a brief description. See table 3.1 for some examples.
- Determine the boundary and scope of your enterprise.
- Clearly articulate your enterprise strategic goals and objectives.
- Select and define the enterprise capabilities required to achieve your goals. Refer to table 3.2.

Questions for consideration

- Have you validated your enterprise mission, ideology, and core values?
- Do you clearly understand the strategic imperatives driving change?
- Who are the constituents in your ecosystem and how do you interact?
- What is the pace of change in your ecosystem?
- What capabilities exist today that can be leveraged?
- What capabilities does your enterprise need to meet future goals?
- How well positioned is your enterprise for possible ecosystem change?

4   Performing Stakeholder Analysis

Value is in the eye of the beholder.

Close examination of the enterprise landscape will have made it abundantly clear that the enterprise has many diverse stakeholders. We now turn to the task of performing a deeper analysis of the stakeholders. Our belief is that you cannot understand stakeholders without taking a value perspective. In fact, the concept of value is central to thinking about the enterprise in a holistic way.

An enterprise exists to deliver value, and value is defined primarily in terms of how it is perceived by the enterprise's stakeholders, and what value they give to and receive from it. The enterprise stakeholders are the people who "reside" within the enterprise, as well as those in its ecosystem who directly or indirectly affect, or are affected by, the level of achievement of the enterprise's objectives and its value-creation processes. Value is how stakeholders perceive utility, benefit, or reward in exchange for their respective contributions to the enterprise.

How Enterprises Create Value

Value creation is not a simple matter in complex enterprises; there are many aspects to this. How does the enterprise effectively focus on things that create value, and avoid doing things that are non–value adding? How can the enterprise create value for its stakeholders given incomplete knowledge, and with limited resources? And how can the enterprise sustain value delivery, given that what stakeholders value today is not always what they may value tomorrow?

In the past, many enterprises focused almost exclusively on financial value and/or on satisfying their customers. Based on research and its application in both industry and government, this has now broadened significantly to encompass value from multiple perspectives, both for and from all stakeholders.[1] Whether the stakeholder is the owner, an employee, a supplier, or a customer, the enterprise must think about value with respect to each stakeholder. Selected parts of the enterprise often put major emphasis on specific stakeholders and minimal emphasis on others. This may be appropriate, but the enterprise perspective needs to consider all stakeholders. Our experience is that value delivery is, unfortunately, all too often conceptualized without a holistic enterprise perspective.

Since creating value is the enterprise's reason for existence, our approach to enterprise architecting adopts a *value-driven perspective*. The emphasis is on how value, as a whole, is created across the enterprise. As the phrase "in exchange" indicates, value is not just unidirectional. The enterprise may value the specific contribution employees make; those employees may value their salary levels and the supportive workplace they enjoy when they come to work each day. The enterprise may value the cost-effective components a particular supplier provides; that supplier may value the financial and other benefits that come from the way the enterprise it supplies does business.

Grounded in its understanding of the enterprise landscape (chapter 3), the architecting team now needs to take a closer look at stakeholders. What do they value individually? What value do they contribute to the enterprise? What are the relationships of value across the enterprise? This value chain needs to be understood. The first step in gaining a holistic understanding of stakeholder value in an enterprise is to identify all the stakeholders (or groups of stakeholders), and what they each value.

Enterprises typically have a host of individual and group stakeholders, and value is enterprise-specific. In some types of enterprises there is a difference between customers and end users. For a consumer-product enterprise they can be one and the same, but in other enterprises this difference can be significant. For instance, an aircraft manufacturer's customers are the airlines that buy its planes, but members of the flying public are the end users. This particular enterprise must ensure that there is a clear understanding of what each group values. Some points of contention are likely to be found in these values. For example, the flying public values legroom when flying, but the airline wants to maximize the number of seats in an aircraft. It is important to understand these conflicting areas of value, so decisions will not inadvertently favor one stakeholder over others.

Each enterprise will have its unique view of which stakeholders are most important. Enterprises most often cite customers as the key group, along with shareholders (or the equivalent). Employees constitute a critical stakeholder group, but they are rarely valued as most important to an enterprise. Southwest Airlines is a notable exception, and its approach has made it highly successful.[2]

The enterprise does not ignore other stakeholders, but it focuses more attention on its employee stakeholders than most enterprises we observe in its market segment. The philosophy at Southwest is that if the company has well-trained, well-paid, highly motivated, and satisfied employees, those employees will, in turn, make Southwest's customers happy and the company will operate more efficiently and effectively. Recent research indicates that a greater focus on stakeholder value (including that of employee stakeholders) rather than shareholder value can end up creating more value for shareholders than the reverse.[3]

Our research has revealed that a significant number of enterprises have never really taken the trouble to actually identify all their stakeholders and what they specifically value. Since this can often be a relatively simple and inexpensive task, it is surprising to find it is often not done. Sometimes this is because it is assumed that all stakeholders are known and understood. Another reason for this is the lack of a next-step approach to use this information to create insights that can be incorporated effectively into enterprise decision making, particularly with an eye to the future. Of course, this activity is not a one-time exercise. It needs to be periodically performed since stakeholders and their perceived value do change over time.

Once the values of each stakeholder group are identified, this knowledge is used to understand the value proposition, which comprises what the enterprise does for a stakeholder, what that stakeholder does for the enterprise, and what they both value. The value proposition can be seen in terms of how value flows across relationships. Value is what flows as stakeholders interact with the enterprise; the value that flows in one direction is compensated by the value flowing in the other direction, as in the case of employees providing services in exchange for pay.

Other examples of stakeholder value and the value flow across relationships might include suppliers who value the invitation to be involved early in the design process of products, so that they can maximize the efficiency of their contribution to the finished work. In turn, the enterprise values the suppliers' commitment to achieving low lifecycle cost and superb quality of parts. The societal stakeholders may value the jobs the enterprise provides in the community, the contributions the enterprise makes to the overall improvement of the community, and the fact that the enterprise considers environmental factors to be an important part of its processes. In turn, the enterprise may value the infrastructure support within the locality that helps sustain the enterprise. Good relations between the enterprise and its local community make it a desirable place for the enterprise's employees to live. Shared value propositions are necessary for high-performing enterprises.

Analysis of Stakeholders

There are numerous techniques the architecting team can use to investigate stakeholder value; some are discussed here and many others may be found in the literature. Prior to the stakeholder analysis, the architecting team will want to select the "tools" it will use in this activity. The team should agree on the stakeholder groups, and on the degree of discussion needed with these groups.

To initiate stakeholder analysis, the architecting team needs to identify who the stakeholders are, prioritize them, and determine how they exchange value with and within the enterprise. This analysis is a prerequisite to understanding the as-is architecture. Typical stakeholder groups for a corporation include

- Customers/end users
- Shareholders
- Employees
- Suppliers
- Partners
- Corporate leadership
- Society
- Unions

Not all of these stakeholders will necessarily be present in every enterprise (e.g., unions), but we find that these groups exist in most enterprises and are similar, with some variations.

The first task after identifying the different groups of stakeholders is to look at their particular needs and perspectives. In doing so, architects must be careful to consider the different "voices" among the most critical stakeholders. This is typically accomplished by interviewing multiple stakeholders in each relevant category (e.g., customers, employees, suppliers, etc.) and/or through the use of existing (recent) data such as employee or customer surveys.

A useful technique for the architecting team is to have a means to ensure there is a degree of commonality in capturing the prioritization for each of the stakeholder groups. Once the team identifies the stakeholders, and analyzes the value exchange between these stakeholders and the enterprise, some simple templates help capture this information.

One effective method of analyzing the value delivered to each stakeholder is through quantifying the importance of each value to them as well as the performance of the enterprise in delivering on each value. This is typically recorded on a simple 1-to-5 scale, as reflected in stakeholder interviews. From this information, it is possible to create simple *value delivery graphs* showing the stakeholder value comparison. The graphs provide a visual depiction of the relative

Table 4.1

Assessing importance and value delivery for the employee stakeholder

Stakeholder group: Employees		
Questions to guide stakeholder conversation: *What does the stakeholder value? What does the stakeholder expect from the enterprise? What would make the stakeholder think highly of the enterprise?*	*How important is this value to this stakeholder group?* 1 = low 5 = high	*How well is the enterprise delivering this value?* 1 = low 5 = high
Fair wages	5	5
Job satisfaction	5	4
Security	2	4
Rewards	4	3
Career growth	5	2
Tools to do the job	4	1
Work facilities	3	1
Training	3	1

importance of values to the stakeholder and the enterprise's delivery on those values to that stakeholder.

For example, consider a large aerospace enterprise that was undergoing a major transformation to reduce product development and delivery times. Table 4.1 shows the aggregated stakeholder value importance and performance information for the employee stakeholder group based on interviewing them. They scored the current value delivery using a simple five-level scale.

This can further be illustrated using the value delivery graph in figure 4.1, which plots the scores displayed in table 4.1. We have found that this simple representation provides a great visual tool for rapidly seeing disconnects in the value expected versus the value delivered to the stakeholder.

Examining this data, the leadership in this aerospace enterprise was pleased to learn that their employees feel they are well paid and like their jobs (upper-right quadrant of figure 4.1). What they really desire is more career-growth opportunities, along with the tools and training to do their jobs (bottom-right quadrant). This is a particularly important insight in light of the need to enhance and possibly introduce new methods of streamlining product development and delivery processes. Additionally, employees would like more recognition for what they do, along with better facilities to work in (although this is slightly less important than the tools and career-growth values). This analysis suggests the future architecture must protect the upper-right-quadrant value delivery (fair wages, job satisfaction) and improve the lower-right, where

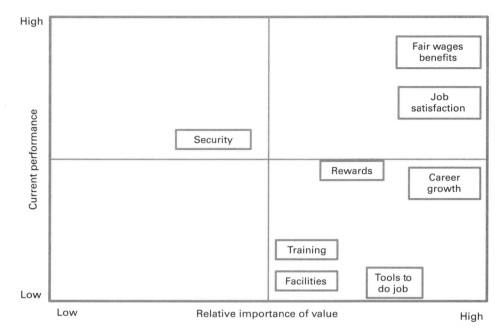

Figure 4.1
Current enterprise performance versus importance of value to employees

importance is high but current enterprise value delivery performance is too low. Security, in the upper-left quadrant, is important but the relative importance is rated as fairly low. The question to ask is whether this is because it is not perceived as highly important since it is taken for granted, or if the enterprise is actually overdelivering on this value. These value exchanges were revisited by the architecting team after completing other stakeholder and process analyses.

Understanding Value Exchanges

Following the gathering of all stakeholder values, the team has the task of analyzing this information to understand the value exchanges. Let's take the case of a healthcare system that recognized the need to assist its now-retired clients requiring healthcare while traveling away from home for an extended period. The care system is organized as a regional network of loosely coupled care centers. The care system serves a population of stakeholders on a national basis, and in general, they require only in-region care. The now-retired stakeholders continue to receive care in the regional system, but may spend months away in another region. For example, some are "snowbirds" living in colder regions who seek warmer climates, and others are those who spend some portion of their time living with family in other locations.

This is a rapidly growing segment of the client base for this healthcare provider, and these clients are unhappy about the difficulty receiving care while traveling to other regions. A sample observation gleaned from an investigation of this issue:

Traveling clients who seek routine care and arrive at distant regional facilities without prior notice may face barriers to timely care. If not registered in that regional center, these clients must first register at the center's eligibility office. Prior to obtaining temporary supplies of routine medications, traveling clients are evaluated by providers at the alternate regional facility who write prescriptions anew, a cumbersome process that may take hours to days to complete.

This growing trend of traveling clients within this healthcare enterprise triggered a transformation initiative to make care across regions a more seamless experience for clients. The first step was to identify the value exchange between the enterprise stakeholders in regard to what is expected and what is contributed. An excerpt from this analysis is shown in table 4.2.

Results of this value-exchange analysis for the *physician* stakeholder group are portrayed in figure 4.2. A review of the survey responses from physicians identified three primary discrepancies between current performance of the enterprise and relative importance of particular values to physicians: ability to locate information within the electronic medical record (EMR); ability to access information within the medical record; and effective communication.

Table 4.2

Healthcare-system stakeholder value exchange (excerpt)

Value expected from enterprise	Stakeholders	Value contributed to enterprise
Medical care when and where needed, with seamless care across regions	Clients	Client subscription to healthcare program, with payment for services
Ability to place, access, and locate accurate information in medical record regardless of region where care is received	Physicians	Medical care to eligible clients, timely updates to medical records, and ordering of tests/ treatments when/where needed
Ability to communicate with regional offices, access centralized medical record, and make timely verification of eligibility	Referral case managers	Managing care process across regions, and ensuring clients understand where to get care within regions

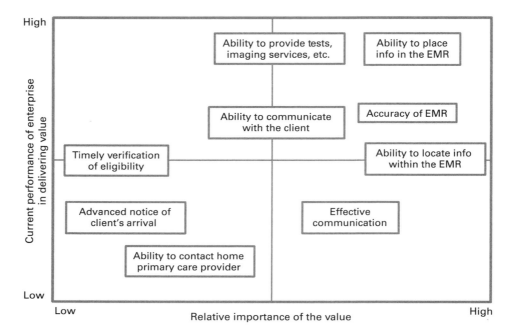

Figure 4.2
Relative importance of value to the physician

Based on this feedback, it appears that this enterprise needs to place greater emphasis on improving access to patients' medical records. Because clients cross regional boundaries, physicians' ability to locate and obtain information from these records across the regions is important. These problems were deemed related to issues in effectively communicating with patients. In a similar analysis for the referral case managers, four values were identified where there was a large discrepancy between current performance and relative importance of these values: effective communication; advance notice of traveling client's arrival; ability to provide consults with a provider; and timely verification of eligibility.

Based on these observed gaps, the team was able to understand the importance of aiding referral case managers as they coordinate client transfer across regions. In contrast to the physician stakeholder group, referral case managers seemed satisfied with the current recordkeeping systems, but were concerned about their ability to communicate in a timely manner with the other stakeholders involved in the cross-regional care process. Value analysis helps in discovering such indicators.

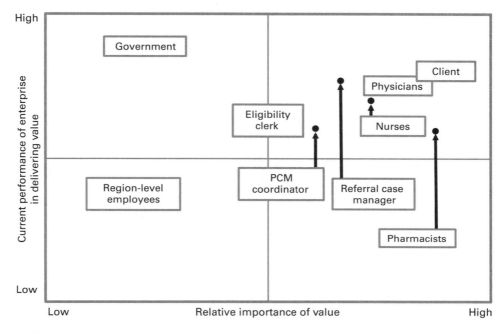

Figure 4.3
Consolidated stakeholder value exchange

Looking at Value Holistically across Stakeholders

After completing similar value analyses for each stakeholder, additional insight is gained by examining how value is being delivered in the aggregate to stakeholders. With the graphs completed for all stakeholders, the value exchange for the entire enterprise can be visualized in yet another value prioritization and delivery graph, as shown in figure 4.3. This depiction can assist in answering such questions as: Which stakeholders are most important? Which are underserved? Do common issues surface across your stakeholder population?

In this case, the stakeholder value elicitation revealed that the performance of the enterprise more closely matched some of the stakeholders' values than others. Based on these results and interviews within the enterprise, the boxes in figure 4.3 present the current value delivery by the enterprise to key stakeholders. Clients and care providers seem well served, while certain other stakeholders (pharmacists, referral case managers, primary-care management (PCM) coordinators, and nurses) are underserved considering their importance to the traveling client. Because referral case managers are ideally supposed to own and manage the client transfer process, this highlights an important deficiency in the current system. Also, pharmacists are crucial to meeting the needs of upward of 30 percent of traveling client care requests. Therefore, the future-state enterprise clearly must serve the needs of these four stakeholders better than it is at present. The upward arrows in figure 4.3 indicate the direction in which the value delivery needs to move in the future-state architecture.

Which Stakeholders Are Most Important?

Further analysis is necessary to enable the team to understand priorities in regard to which stakeholders should be listened to most, and which should be served to a greater extent, in the particular enterprise transformation initiative. While it is useful to broadly gather stakeholder knowledge from across the enterprise (and sometimes the larger ecosystem), this information has the potential to bias the decisions of the team, unless some relative weights are put on the voices heard during the stakeholder analysis. That is, prioritizing stakeholders is very important, because not all stakeholders have the same importance to the enterprise.

One of the most important roles the architecting team brings to the stakeholder analysis is that of performing "objective analysis" to the extent possible given the qualitative nature of the analysis. Simple approaches are effective, although sometimes teams may want to use a more extensive technique. A useful one that applies this objectivity is to map and understand *stakeholder salience,* and use this information to better shape enterprise change.

Stakeholder salience is based on three stakeholder attributes.[4] The first is power. Powerful stakeholders possess power in relation to the enterprise and so may be capable of imposing their will on it. The CEO of a corporation and a commanding officer in the military are two examples of powerful stakeholders. The second attribute is legitimacy—that is, the perception that the actions of a stakeholder are desirable, proper, or appropriate within the norms, values, and beliefs of the enterprise. A well-respected, experienced chief engineer is an example of a legitimate stakeholder. Finally, urgency exists when the stakeholder's relationship with the enterprise is time-sensitive and/or is of importance to strategy and operations. For example, in the event of an aircraft engine failure, the government investigator would be an urgent stakeholder. Determining stakeholder salience is thus about asking three important questions: What power does the stakeholder have to influence the enterprise? How legitimate is the stakeholder's relationship with the enterprise? How critical is the stakeholder's claim on the enterprise? Stakeholder salience is defined by the cumulative number of and intensity of these three attributes.

The answers to these questions provide the team with a way to categorize stakeholders into one of three groups. Definitive stakeholders are those that possess all three attributes. Expectant stakeholders possess any two of the three attributes. Latent stakeholders possess one attribute.[5] The definitive and expectant stakeholders are key, but latent stakeholders cannot be ignored. The bottom line is that when prioritizing, all salient stakeholders must be accounted for, since they can influence outcomes significantly. Recent research has investigated the strong relationship between enterprise architecture, stakeholder salience, and the creation of enterprise value.[6]

One example we observed was a case of an enterprise undergoing a transformation targeted at outsourcing the manufacturing of component parts (presently developed in-house) as part of a new business strategy. The architecting team placed significant focus on who they saw as the 'powerful stakeholders' making decisions and managing the suppliers, but it failed to sufficiently listen to the voice of the people on the manufacturing shop floor. While they talked with these individuals about fair treatment in termination of jobs in the enterprise, the team neglected to capture their expert opinions on how to effectively transition from in-house manufacture of parts to the procurement of parts while keeping the line running. Failing to do so introduced uncertainties and risk that might have been avoided, and resulted in delays in delivery of the manufactured end product during the transition that took place over an eighteen-month period. Perhaps if the architecting team had used saliency analysis, it would have decided to spend more time on the shop floor.

Relationship of Stakeholder Values to View Elements

One additional technique we use to probe more deeply at what stakeholders value is to look at the relative importance of the view elements (introduced in chapter 2) for each stakeholder. Table 4.3 provides an example where relative

Table 4.3
Importance of views for each stakeholder (H—high, M—medium, L—low).

	Strategy	Organization	Process	Knowledge	Infrastructure
Purchasers	M	H	L	M	L
Insurers	M	H	L	M	L
Providers	H	H	M	H	M
Suppliers	M	M	L	M	L
Regulators	L	H	M	M	L

importance was assessed based on the surveys and interviews the architecting team conducted with the stakeholders of a hospital healthcare system. In this case, the importance was ranked as high, medium, and low; some teams use a 1-to-5 scale. It is not really the scale that matters, but the ability to discern relative importance. This could be done by asking the stakeholders to indicate the importance of various items in a table like this, but our experience is that it is more effective for the team to make this assessment, because the individual stakeholders may not fully understand what is encompassed in each view element. So, what does this information reveal? First, it may show where further discussions are merited as the team moves forward into the transformation. Second, patterns may emerge. In the example in table 4.3 we can see that the organization view is perceived as high by the purchasers, insurers, providers, and regulators in this enterprise, but of this subgroup, only the providers see knowledge as having high importance. Such patterns can lead to additional questions. For example, what drives the importance of knowledge for providers? It could be that they have an unfulfilled need or critical dependence on having the latest medical knowledge to treat their patients. It is important to understand which it is.

Assessing the relative significance of the view elements is another way to get a big-picture understanding of what the stakeholders value, and where that value delivery may be lacking. And any deeper understanding gained in such an analysis will be important when considering alternatives for the future.

Changing Stakeholder Values over Time

As the team looks to understand stakeholder values, it is critical to remember that enterprises operate in an increasingly complex environment where different uncertainties arise over time. External context factors—economy, markets, prices, competitors, regulations, technologies, and so on—can change and affect the actual and perceived value delivery. Needs and values change over time, as does the set of enterprise stakeholders itself. In other words, because the world is not static, stakeholder value creation must be dynamic and iterative. As an enterprise expands into new markets, there may be all sorts of new stakeholders, such as customers, regulators, and new employee populations. As technology changes, what stakeholders want and need can alter drastically. For example, customers purchasing mobile phones today value very different features than those popular five years ago, and desirable features are certain to be much different five years into the future. This is just one example of how stakeholders and stakeholder value are dynamic. The architecting team needs to investigate such potential value shifts.

Value and context are linked. The enterprise context serves to shape the stakeholder value at any given time, as well as the ability of the enterprise to deliver value. Hence, the link between value and context is inextricable. However, one must keep in mind that a stakeholder may not be aware of many aspects of the broader enterprise. Stakeholder input, as important as it is to identifying everything architects need to know about value, may be limited by the stakeholder's relatively narrow perspective. Some stakeholders may never grasp, for instance, that there are constraints on the ability to manufacture in a given region, or that there is a cap set by the board of directors on how much can be invested by the enterprise in certain areas. Input from stakeholders is important, but the architecting team must be aware that stakeholders often do not see the full set of broader enterprise needs.

Pulling Together Stakeholder-Related Insights

The process of identifying stakeholders, prioritizing them, and eliciting the value exchange between the stakeholders and the enterprise is a critical step in developing a holistic picture of how the enterprise creates value. The value-exchange analysis must account for bidirectional value flows from the stakeholder to the enterprise and from the enterprise to the stakeholder. Additionally, further understanding stakeholder importance using saliency analysis enables the enterprise to better comprehend the nature and dynamics of value exchange, both for today and, more importantly, for what may be required in the future. This understanding can be further enhanced by examining stakeholder value through the view elements. All in all, an investigation of this nature provides important insights for designing a future architecture to maximize value delivery to stakeholders. This entails a balancing act, and knowledge gained in this analysis supports judgment calls that will need to be made.

Once the analysis is complete, the team will want to spend some time synthesizing what was learned. A composite picture of enterprise stakeholders will emerge, and this will feed forward into the next activity, capturing the current architecture.

Performing Stakeholder Analysis

Exercises to apply to your own enterprise

- Identify each of your enterprise stakeholders.
- Using the templates in table 4.2 and figure 4.2, determine the value exchange for each stakeholder.
- Determine the relative importance of each stakeholder, as illustrated in figure 4.3.

Questions for consideration

- Which stakeholders are most important for your overall enterprise?
- Will any stakeholders become more/less important over time?
- What shifts in stakeholder value delivery are important for the future?
- Are there new stakeholders that will be important in the future?
- What view elements are most critical to consider in designing for future value delivery?
- Does the architecting team have representatives who can view the enterprise from the perspective of stakeholders?

5   Capturing the Current Architecture

If you don't understand the existing enterprise, you cannot be sure you are architecting a better one.

Architecting the future enterprise means launching from the current enterprise, except for the special case where an entirely new enterprise is being designed. Architecting depends on understanding the enterprise as it presently exists and functions. This is simple common sense. If the architecting team does not understand the point of departure for making changes, effective transitions may not be possible. If architects fail to understand current strengths and capabilities, the new architecture may fail to retain those that will still be advantageous in the future. Without sufficient knowledge of the past history and present state of the enterprise to build on, the plan for the future may prove unsuitable for the enterprise given its legacy, its culture, and the way it functions as part of its ecosystem.

It would be easy to make the assumption that the current enterprise is fully understood without investing effort, but this would be a mistake. Seldom does any single individual understand all the interconnections and relationships across the enterprise. An enterprise, as a living system, is always changing and architects need up-to-date knowledge.

Sometimes enterprise change is intentional—for example, as a result of targeted improvement initiatives or planned changes in the product line. The need for change may also arise suddenly and must be addressed. An unplanned but necessary workforce reduction due to a sudden economic downturn is an example. The urgency of the latter situation puts pressure on the architecting team to move to a solution. Regardless of the situation, the architects must take the time to capture the present situation. Stepping back and investigating the current state of the enterprise is well worth the investment of time and effort.

At this point in the architecting process, the team has already begun its efforts to understand the current state through the investigation of the enterprise landscape, both internal and external (its ecosystem). Stakeholder analysis has been completed, as we discussed in chapter 4. Building on this understanding, we turn to the eight view elements. Before a future can be effectively envisioned, the as-is architecture must be properly investigated and captured to reveal a holistic picture of the enterprise today.

Enterprise Elements as Lenses

The enterprise elements serve as useful lenses to compose a picture of the whole enterprise.[1] Our research has shown that some elements will be more important than others in the design of a given future architecture, though all are important to the enterprise at large. When designing a new architecture, we recommend following a specific order in employing the elements (we discuss this in chapter 8). When using the elements to describe the current architecture, however, we find that a specific order is not really necessary. In fact, spiraling through the elements multiple times is helpful. The key reason for using the unique perspectives provided by the elements is to make tractable the task of seeing the whole enterprise.[2] The elements need to be described individually, but the architecting team also needs to discover the interrelationships among the elements, and where relationships between elements should exist but do not. All of this information will inform the future architecture.

The enterprise element model (introduced in chapter 2) provides a useful descriptive tool for capturing the current architecture, and also frames the dialogue with enterprise stakeholders to explore different aspects of the current enterprise. This model contains the various elements that can be used to compose a "picture" of the enterprise that is easily communicated to the sponsor, and to others who have a reviewing role. By this, we mean a vivid architectural description using the enterprise elements to tell a story. Let's look at some sample descriptors from a recent architecting case.

Solar Solutions Case

Solar Solutions is a growing company in the energy sector, located in the Northeastern region of the United States. The company develops and services solar energy products. Table 5.1 provides simple descriptive statements about Solar Solutions as an enterprise, for each of the ten enterprise elements.

As can be seen, both positive and negative characteristics are enumerated. We show just one descriptor for each element in the table; this architecting team would have elaborated multiple descriptors for each element. Elaborating on each element using the element anatomy could then be used to enrich the current enterprise description.

Table 5.1

Selected element examples for Solar Solutions

Element	Illustrative examples from the Solar Solutions enterprise
Ecosystem	Solar Solutions is currently the market leader in its region, but several new competitors have recently emerged that may take market share.
Stakeholder	Suppliers are essential partners in providing installation service, but Solar Solutions does not currently measure customer satisfaction with this service.
Strategy	Solar Solutions intends to expand globally within the next two years, yet still has not investigated target markets.
Information	Marketing gathers consumer needs for product enhancements, but product managers do not always receive these in a timely manner.
Infrastructure	Solar Solutions's information technology systems do not work well together, but each functional area seems to have what they require.
Products	The Solar Solutions product family is based on two product platforms, each having several variants to satisfy diversity of needs in the market.
Services	Customer service appears to operate separately from product development, resulting in communication delays in problem reporting.
Process	Solar Solutions has five relatively mature and effective core business processes, but their lack of integration creates some inefficiencies and duplication of effort.
Organization	Organizational boundaries between teams developing product components tend to be barriers to effective collaboration.
Knowledge	Far too much of Solar Solutions's intellectual property is accessible only via a gatekeeper in the senior leadership.

As illustrated in this case, all elements contribute to an understanding of an enterprise, but they may not all be equally important for a particular transformation initiative. The ecosystem and stakeholder elements are almost always of high importance. It is our experience that the remaining eight elements may fall into several tiers of importance as applied to the transformation initiative. Simply put, elements could be deemed highly important, moderately important, or not very important. It can be challenging to rank-order all eight view elements, but discussions with key stakeholders may reveal which elements most heavily drive stakeholder value given the change the enterprise is undertaking. That said, the element or elements representing the major driver in the as-is enterprise may not be the most important going forward.

Enterprise Element Anatomy

Our research has led to an approach for looking deeper at the eight view elements from a "parts" perspective. We refer to this as the *element anatomy*. The value of the anatomy is to provide architects with a schema to "look under the covers." The five parts of the element anatomy are structure, behavior, artifacts, measures, and periodicity. Such information can be uncovered through discussions with stakeholders. As an example, the *artifacts* are "tangible evidence" of characteristics of the enterprise. For instance, the annual report an enterprise produces is an artifact where a rich set of information can be found. Process document libraries and process maps are obvious examples of process-related artifacts. The artifact many enterprises present when asked to describe their enterprise is a formal organizational chart.

Our research has shown that the anatomy can reveal unique information that is driven by the type of enterprise. The quantification of performance is important to any enterprise, and most enterprises generally have measures for this purpose, whether explicit or implicit (unstated but generally accepted and understood). The actual measures, and whether these are effective in promoting a desired outcome, are highly variable. Market share will be an important measure in a commercial enterprise, but not for a public school. Standard profit measures will be explicit measures in a for-profit enterprise, but not in a public agency. Compliance with regulatory restrictions would be an obvious measure related to the product and service elements in a highly regulated industry sector. The pace of the regulatory environment may change frequently or slowly in different industries.

Table 5.2 describes the anatomy of the organization element for a large commercial software product enterprise. Looking at the enterprise through each element and its anatomical parts permits deeper insights. The enterprise was configured by major business functions (*structure*) and exhibited high degrees of collaboration given the tone set by leadership (*behavior*) across these functional areas. In this investigation, seven levels of management (*measure*) were described to us, and also evidenced by the formal organizational chart (*artifact*) that documented these levels. When we investigated further, we found that most decisions were rapid, but it typically took over four weeks to get a software change request approved (*periodicity*). Characterizing the element through its anatomy strengthens understanding. Such information can be used to compose descriptive enterprise vignettes to describe the current enterprise.

Assessing Element Importance and Interrelationships

During its early investigation, the architecting team can explore the question of whether each of the view elements is likely to become more or less important

Table 5.2

Element anatomy with select examples

	Description	Example
Structure	Configuration characteristics	Organization element structure could be functional versus matrix, flat, or hierarchical.
Behavior	Responses to certain conditions or triggers	Repeatability of processes could be process element behavior as a result of standardization of the processes.
Artifacts	Tangible evidence	Strategy element artifacts could include an annual report, technology roadmaps, and strategic plans.
Measures	Quantitative information	Knowledge element measures could be percent of patents granted of all submitted.
Periodicity	Recurring cycles, both with pace and rate	Strategy element periodicity could be strategic planning cycle intervals (e.g., annual or every five years).

in the future. An enterprise that has mature business processes with a stable workforce may be dominated by the process element, for example, but its future architecture could require greater attention to another element. Major personnel turnovers or high attrition could make the knowledge element higher priority in the future architecture, because a largely novice workforce will need to be trained to understand and perform standard processes. In other words, the enterprise could have the best processes in the world, but if the knowledge to execute those processes is on its way out the door, the enterprise could be headed for failure. In the enterprise's future architecture, the knowledge element may need the most attention. This back-and-forth between present and future is an important part of the thinking the team needs to do.

As this discussion of elements might suggest, the description of the current architecture needs to determine how the elements interrelate.[3] Of course, at some level, it is likely that everything relates to everything else. The architecting team has a critical task here, in that the key element relationships and dependencies must be uncovered. It is not always obvious what these are, and it may take some investigation and deep thinking on the part of the team. In short, the most visible element-to-element relationships are not always the most important.

Understanding Drivers and Impacts

The strategic imperatives for change (as discussed in chapter 3), both past and present, are central to understanding the enterprise as it exists today. The architecting team needs to understand the major issues and uncertainties that the enterprise faces. Often, beyond the explicitly stated strategic imperatives and objectives of the senior leadership voiced to the architecting team, answers can be found by examining the artifacts the enterprise produces and those others produce about the enterprise. Annual reports show facts and figures, and also aspirations and stretch goals. Market survey data may reveal successes and short-falls. Internal surveys can provide a plethora of information about the culture, and about where things work well and where they do not.

The enterprise's website may be interesting to examine. Websites typically reveal a lot about the culture and how the collective enterprise thinks. The team can find some good soft indicators here. Does it reveal dominant elements? Does it reveal key enterprise capabilities (e.g., evidence of agility, sustainability, etc.)? Does it show a culture that cares about people, the environment, and/or share-holders? Unique insights may be gained by examining the face the enterprise chooses to show the world through its online persona, as well as in other artifacts such as annual reports.

Direct customer feedback and interviews with stakeholders do, of course, also provide insight. The value of stakeholder input about current conditions cannot be overstated. Imagine asking the relevant stakeholders about the extent to which they feel they are given decision-making authority and resources to drive change in the organization. Then, imagine how the architecture might be modi-fied to provide authority and resources where these are needed but presently lacking.

The impact of the enterprise in its operating environment can also be explored through secondary sources. Media reports may reveal how well the enterprise is doing or how others see the enterprise in relation to similar enterprises. There may be evidence of recent actions, like layoffs or rapid hiring or receipt of a key industry prize. The impact of the enterprise on its competitors may also be evident in media or trade reports that discuss market share. Looking at trends is another potential source of insights—for example, the enterprise may have gained or lost market share during the past several years.

Composing a clear picture of the as-is architecture reveals the "gaps" that a future architecture may need to fill. In fact, a specific gap analysis is part of capturing the current architecture. Our research has shown that some of the deficiencies include misalignment of performance measures with strategic objec-tives, weak relationships across certain elements, or a failure to deliver the value the enterprise stakeholders require.

The current enterprise can suffer from various design flaws. For instance, a poorly designed employee incentive program can lead to high attrition rates. Lack of competitive health benefits may reduce the desired flow of potential new hires. Countless enterprises may, at some point, find a hiring freeze affects critical skill needs. At the same time, changes in strategy result in excesses such as employees with outdated skills, or too many middle managers. An overly constrained or shortsighted R&D program, for example, may limit innovation, making the products obsolete as the world changes.

The architecting team will also want to further explore the enterprise capabilities (chapter 3). Understanding current capabilities, and their value to stakeholders, informs what it will take to strengthen these capabilities, or alternatively, to go in a different direction. A growing enterprise, for instance, may lack workforce scalability—that is, the capability to scale up or scale back the workforce as market demand changes. Creating an architecture to effectively accommodate outsourcing and/or the use of temporary employees might be appropriate to consider for the future if workforce scalability is deemed important.

Capturing information uncovered by the team can take various forms. Using graphics can be helpful, especially in mapping relationships among the elements. It is also very important to describe the current characteristics of relevant "soft factors" such as culture, trust, openness, and loyalty. The positive soft factors and effective practices should probably be retained in the new architecture if they are aligned with future enterprise goals. The future architecture may need to target reversal of soft factors that are less than optimal, and improve ineffective and inefficient practices.

This investigation is essential to understanding not only the current situation of the enterprise, but also how it got there. How did the organization grow? What does the enterprise value? What have its successes and failures been over time? Exploring the history of the enterprise can provide valuable insights into what success will mean in the envisioned future (we discuss creating the envisioned future in chapter 6). The team needs a comprehensive assessment of the current enterprise to know what to change, and equally important, what to keep.

Using SWOT Analysis

A simple and effective technique to use in organizing the results of the current-state investigation is SWOT or a similar tool. A well-known business technique, SWOT stands for Strengths, Weaknesses, Opportunities, and Threats. A SWOT analysis involves identifying the factors, both external and internal, that are either favorable or unfavorable to achieving a given objective. In SWOT nomenclature, and as we use the term here in regard to enterprise assessment, *strength* refers to characteristics that give the enterprise an advantage over others or enable it to achieve challenging goals and strategic objectives. Strengths can be everything from a good reputation with customers to favorable access to a distribution network to patents to proprietary know-how. For a nonprofit enterprise, a strength could be that the enterprise has existing relationships with generous philanthropists, whose donations allow it to fulfill its mission. For a government agency, a strength may be its ability to attract top talent, even though salaries the enterprise can offer are below those in the private sector.

A *weakness* places the enterprise at a disadvantage relative to others, or is a root cause of the enterprise's failure to achieve its strategic objectives. It may be the flipside of strength, as in the case of having a large workforce with lots of embedded knowledge of the enterprise's industry. That strength could possibly translate into a weakness because of the cost of maintaining an extensive workforce. Other weaknesses are things such as a poor reputation among customers, a lack of access to distribution channels, a weak brand name, and so on. A weakness in a charitable organization could be the lack of information technology infrastructure required to efficiently run its operations. In a government agency, it could be an ineffective leadership-succession planning process, resulting in delays in critical decisions.

Opportunities and threats take an outward-looking perspective. An *opportunity* is an external chance to succeed in the enterprise's broader environment. For instance, a new technology may be on the horizon, and the enterprise has already figured out a way to capture the potential for profit and growth from employing it once it becomes available. An invitation to become the first vendor in an emerging economy might be an opportunity (although one should be able to imagine some pitfalls, too). An unfulfilled need in the marketplace almost always represents an opportunity.

Finally, there is the *threat*, which is something in the ecosystem that could cause trouble for the enterprise. What if consumers no longer have a need for the products made by the enterprise, because a new disruptive technology provides a better and less expensive option? That, of course, could threaten the enterprise's very existence. New policies, regulations, and trade barriers are also types of threats that affect commercial, government, and not-for-profit enterprises.

SWOT Analysis: An Illustrative Case

Using the view elements as lenses can provide a way to enrich a SWOT analysis, as illustrated by a simplified example involving the Starbucks Corporation.[4] This highly successful enterprise provides a good example because many of the strengths, weaknesses, opportunities, and threats, taken from the perspective of its elements, will be familiar to readers.

Consider the product element. For Starbucks, the product element has a strong link to the strategy, service, and process elements. Starbucks offers a range of products and has a high level of employee engagement in offering those products. Products are delivered in alignment with the enterprise's sustainability initiative. Starbucks is committed to ensuring quality, consistency, experience, trust, and loyalty, all components of its service element. Quality and consistency depend on processes (part of the process element).

A quick SWOT analysis of the Starbucks product element yielded the following. Strengths include scalability, customer access, and flexibility. Weaknesses include cost to the consumer of Starbucks coffee (as compared with some other coffee restaurants). Opportunities include a growing demand for customization for customers, the possibility of partnering with other companies on products, and future products that could appeal to the high-end segment of the Starbucks marketplace. Finally, the threats relate to the perceived uniqueness of products given increasing competitors in the marketplace. Starbucks focuses its services on enhancing the customer's experience in multiple ways, for instance, providing appealing stores with comfortable seating and free wireless service. The movement into grocery stores and kiosks, while strengthening product sales, could be a weakness in regard to the perception of the company as a high-end service provider. An opportunity is inherent in sustainability branding for consumers, who are becoming more and more environmentally conscious. The increasing number of competitors and the low barriers to entry for competitors (such as McCafe[5]) may be threats. The service element is linked to strategy, because services are the execution of strategy; to process, because services are executed through processes; and to products, given tight integration of product and service at Starbucks.

In capturing the as-is enterprise, SWOT analysis informs the envisioned future, and will later be used to inspire ideas for generating architectural concepts (chapter 7).

Medical Clinic Case

One of the enterprises we studied was a medical clinic serving the health and wellness needs of a small community. The architecting team investigated the landscape, performed stakeholder analysis, and captured current enterprise information through the lenses of the elements. The primary method in gathering information was through twenty-five detailed interviews with both internal and external stakeholders. These interviews were conducted utilizing a standard interview sheet, but allowed the stakeholder to expand on any issue. Each interview lasted approximately an hour. Various leaders provided the architecting team with additional sources of information. The team also discovered information by looking at the clinic's website, organizational charts, external audit scores, financial information, and annual reports. A brief summary of the current state as captured by this team follows.

Strategy

The health clinic's strategy has received increasing emphasis from the leadership in the last twelve months. In late 2011, the clinic kicked off a new strategic planning cycle by setting up and supporting an architecting team. Five strategic objectives were obtained from the clinic's most recent annual report: (1) access to care, (2) clinical quality, (3) community wellness, (4) managing healthcare costs, and (5) diversity and inclusion.

The architects completed a SWOT analysis and developed four scenarios that the clinic must be equipped to handle in the future, representing four focus areas in the team's analysis. These focus areas include access to care, clinical quality and excellence, community wellness and population health, and expansion. The strategy of this enterprise, as observed from the team's investigation, was not a dominant element in the architecture of the medical clinic, but the organization realizes the importance of a strong strategy.

Infrastructure

The healthcare clinic has two locations: the main facilities in the city it serves, and another healthcare center located in a specific suburb near the city. The main center provides complete healthcare services for all eligible members. The secondary center provides primary care, pediatrics, laboratory, radiology, and support services to members of the community who live or work in the area. Both centers contain similar information technology and communication technologies that make relatively low use of available state-of-the-art resources.

Throughout our analysis we have found that, while the physical facilities are aligned with the current strategy of the enterprise, the IT and communication technologies were applied over enterprise processes and procedures that had important inefficiency levels. Not only were the processes these technologies supported not optimal, but they did not take advantage of the information access or the advanced communication and information technologies available to the enterprise.

Process

The process element is strong in the existing clinic. Because of the clinic's nature as a medical facility, the processes have a controlling effect on the rest of the architecture. Stakeholders were asked about the importance of the various processes in the enterprise and which processes could be improved. The resulting data enabled the team to decide where to focus process improvement initiatives.

In assessing alignment (we discuss this later in the chapter), it was found that while the processes were a dominant element, they are poorly tracked with the important metrics for the organization.

Products

The healthcare clinic is primarily a service provider. The architecting team considered the health plans offered by the clinic to be its primary products. The two health plans are as follows:

- *Basic Health Plan.* This plan includes both the medical plan and an extended insurance plan, which "meets state requirements for comprehensive health insurance."
- *Premium Health Plan.* This plan includes the Basic Health Plan, with additional coverage for wellness and alternative medicine care, along with vision care.

In summary, the two health plan products offer a choice to the community while still being manageable by the enterprise. At this time, there appear to be no major issues with the health plan product offerings.

Services

Regardless of plan, the healthcare clinic provides services to a wide range of clients, including adults, children, and other dependents. The clinic strives to provide consistent care or to improve on existing standards and quality of care every year. The primary services provided include community wellness, dental care, mental health services, vision care, and a customer service support line. Given all these services, the key aspect is customer service level, which has been stable over the years. However, leadership would like to strive for higher standards of customer satisfaction, which is currently tracked through direct feedback.

Knowledge

As with any medical enterprise, knowledge is a very important element. The strength and quality of care provided to the community are directly proportional to the quality of the entire clinical staff of doctors, nurses, nurse-practitioners, medical assistants, and lab technicians. This requires extensive training and credentialing systems to ensure sufficient knowledge to operate the medical enterprise and retain its accreditation.

While having the required knowledge in the organization is important, equally important is the need to ensure it is properly used. The lifecycle process of "standards of care management and application" turned up in the stakeholder survey as one of the most important processes, and one that could most benefit from improvement. The name of this process was changed to "consistent care processes" to avoid a similar legal term. Through the knowledge view, the team investigated the means by which knowledge is brought into the enterprise, synthesized, and promulgated, and determined what was considered important and worthy of further analysis. As a result, a focused effort was undertaken to better understand the stakeholder issue demonstrated in this area.

Organization

The enterprise organizational charts showed the medical director as the director at the top of both charts, assisted in his clinical supervision duties by the associate medical director. From there, each of the clinical areas has its own suborganization. These areas include dentistry, pediatrics, nursing, and mental health, among others. The finance director reports to the medical director as well. On the administrative side, the executive director is responsible for the oversight of information systems, human resources, and operations.

Assessing Enterprise Alignment

As a final step in capturing information about the current enterprise, the architecting team will want to assess alignment. We find a technique called the *X-matrix* effective for this purpose.[6] The X-matrix looks for areas of strong and weak alignment between the enterprise's strategic objectives, performance measures, stakeholder values, and enterprise processes.

It is critical that the strategic objectives be representative of key stakeholder values, and that these values are created in the enterprise processes. Additionally, the enterprise performance measures must be designed to both assess the performance of the strategic objectives and to measure the processes themselves. The X-matrix allows the architecting team to assess whether there is a strong (dark box), a weak (light box), or no (blank box) relationship among these areas. Not every box in the matrix needs to be filled; it is the job of the architecting team to consider where there are weak relationships that need to be strengthened or a missing relationship where one is needed. Any identified misalignment areas present key opportunities for consideration in the future architecture design.

Consider the case of the medical clinic, described above, that serves the health and wellness needs of a small community. When investigating the current state of the enterprise, the X-matrix (figure 5.1) enabled visualization of the misalignments of current metrics with one of the strategic objectives, "Manage healthcare costs," which has only one weak relationship to one single metric. Additionally, it can be seen that several key processes do not have any link to measures (see the bottom-left quadrant). The power of this technique is in providing the team

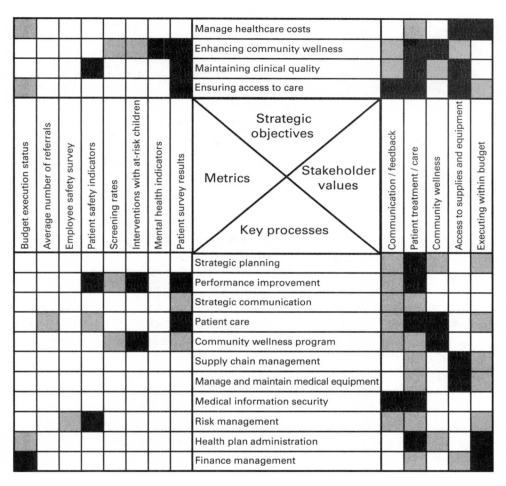

Figure 5.1
Current-state X-matrix for health clinic

with a big-picture perspective, making it possible to systematically examine relationships.

Our research has shown that the alignment of strategic objectives, metrics, processes, and stakeholder values is crucial to overall enterprise performance. In the case above, one clear task for the architecting team will be to address the lack of metrics in the current architecture.

We revisit the *X-matrix* in chapter 9, to assess alignment for the future architecture and to confirm that alignment issues have been resolved where necessary. The architecting team must always be on the lookout for lack of alignment in the enterprise.

Readiness to Envision the Future Enterprise

Understanding an enterprise involves working with a "moving target," so in theory, current-state analysis could go on indefinitely. Practically speaking, as we previously discussed, the team will have determined a stopping point for the investigation of the as-is enterprise. This could be a point when an agreed-on knowledge of various aspects is deemed adequate, or it may simply be a specific date. More often than not it turns out to be the latter even if the former was the original intention. Enterprise leadership and architecting teams need to realize that the investigation of the current enterprise will be performed with incomplete information. It is worth noting the areas where the greatest uncertainty and gaps exist in this analysis. This will help the team at a later point when it attempts to identify any potential risks in the implementation plan. Additionally, this approach may inform the team whether some remedial investigation of the current-state enterprise may be merited later in the architecting effort.

It is wise to hold a formal review activity to determine if there is sufficient information to proceed to the next activity, envisioning the future enterprise. A review also serves to get everyone on the same page with a shared understanding of the current architecture, and a consensus that certain risks inherent in incomplete knowledge need to be accepted. This review is the time to make sure assumptions and rationales are recorded, and that the team sees a clear path for moving forward to the next step in the ARIES process: creating a holistic vision of the future.

Capturing the Current Architecture

Exercises to apply to your own enterprise

- Describe the current state for each view element as shown in table 5.1 and determine the relative importance.
- Perform a SWOT analysis for your enterprise.
- Develop the detailed anatomy for each view element as illustrated in table 5.2.
- Characterize the interrelationships between the views. Consider using a graph or sketch.

Questions for consideration

- Has the as-is architecture been investigated from the perspective of each of the ten elements? From each of the stakeholders?
- Which of the eight view elements are most important in your enterprise? Which seem most interrelated? How do you weight the importance of the relationships?
- What view elements and element relationships in your enterprise may become more or less important over time?
- Has the team checked the alignment of the strategic objectives, metrics, processes, and stakeholder values?

6   Creating a Holistic Vision of the Future

A vision is a dream with a plan.
—Clay Mathilde

Articulating changes for the future depends on a clear understanding of the enterprise as it exists today. A sense of where leadership hopes to take the enterprise, including any shift in business strategy, provides the basis for the envisioned future. The best available information about the enterprise landscape, including impending or anticipated changes in the ecosystem, will influence shaping a realistic and realizable envisioned future state for the enterprise.

A very important question framing the envisioned future is what the time horizon is for this enterprise transformation. Very likely, this information was given to the architecting team at the start, but it's worth confirming it with leadership before this activity begins. It is entirely possible that something has changed in the interim (economic factors, competitive pressures, etc.) that might suggest modifying the time horizon for completing the transformation.

Time Horizon

The transformation time horizon influences choices of strategies the enterprise can invoke to achieve its vision. These strategies likely impose constraints on the transformation plan. Imagine, for example, an enterprise with a five-year time horizon for a transformation focused on a growth strategy that requires three significant acquisitions within eighteen months. Given the investment needed for acquisitions, a realistic future vision is likely to defer other costly initiatives, such as replacement of infrastructure, until a later point in the five-year transformation period.

Time horizons may also introduce uncertainties related to the nature of the enterprise, urgency of the transformation, windows of opportunity, and many other factors. A healthcare provider, for example, may have a pretty good grasp of the services stakeholders will want over a five-year horizon. An enterprise in the fast-paced market of personal technology devices is more likely to take a two-year horizon. For that enterprise, any longer horizon may be unreasonable because knowing what stakeholders will want becomes less and less certain given the rapid and disruptive innovations typical in this business sector.

Time is always a factor in what is possible, and in what is simply infeasible. A two-year window (or even longer) may be a reasonable timeframe for a major organizational transformation in a large established enterprise. It takes time to move a large enterprise. A small start-up, on the other hand, may be able to undertake a transformation every six to twelve months. The architecting team needs to consider maturity and scale of enterprises in creating the vision. It is natural that a more mature enterprise has established policy and processes that take longer to change than those of a new enterprise. Similarly, a smaller enterprise can generally expect to move more quickly than a larger enterprise, simply because fewer people will be involved in a transformation. The future vision must be both "visionary" and grounded in some practical realism.

Context factors—economic, political, regulatory, market, available technology, demographics, and other factors—play an important role in formulating the vision. The team needs to understand, to the extent possible, if new factors and influences will be encountered within the transformation time horizon. For example, if it is expected that environmental concerns will become increasingly important to stakeholders, it will be wise to reflect that in your holistic vision.

Creating a holistic vision of the future requires thinking from multiple perspectives. Here, enterprise view elements, and interactions between these elements, provide lenses to elaborate a vision with various dimensions. For example, if you strive to create a "greener" enterprise, it is important to think not only about how this relates to products, but also to other elements. How will you flow this "green" concept to suppliers? What needs to be done to educate a "green" workforce? Are new organizational roles needed? What policies need to change to produce "green" products? Will it take longer to manufacture a "green" product?

In the investigation of the current enterprise, recall that our architecting team will have identified important enterprise capabilities (e.g., scalability, agility). Now the team needs to ask which capabilities that the enterprise presently possesses will be more or less important to the future enterprise. A start-up company may trace much of its early success and growth to agility. As that same company matures, perhaps with a future vision to expand globally, replicability may surpass agility in importance. Fast growth will become less important than growing in a way that ensures new business units have business practices, policies, and products consistent with those of existing units.

Capturing the Envisioned Future

As should now be apparent, the process of creating a holistic vision of the future is not as simple as putting a pen to paper to record a vision statement. There are all sorts of considerations that must be weighed and accounted for in the creation of a rich transformation vision. Time horizon, enterprise culture, ecosystem factors, and enterprise capabilities must all be considered. Additionally, the future vision should be consistent with the enterprise mission and purpose. Wrapping the various considerations into a concise statement is a first step in articulating an envisioned future. Perhaps it might look something like this:

Our commitment to social and environmental issues is reflected in the 28 countries on all five continents where we operate, and aims at spreading our vision of sustainability in the conduct of the business, always in accordance with local cultures and in a climate of cooperation that enriches us with new experiences.

What you have just read portrays a vision at the highest level. It describes the enterprise at some point down the road and is the overarching expression of what the enterprise architecting effort is aimed at making possible. It is how the enterprise envisions the way its stakeholders will see it following the transformation.

Every enterprise architecting effort requires a clear vision of where the enterprise wants to be in the future. That vision must reflect the strategic objectives that motivate the architecting effort in the first place. It is often first articulated in a complete statement and elaborated on by adding details. Consider this concise statement used by an enterprise that manages high-tech electronic systems as a contractor at a small airport:

We drive value by effectively balancing resources and workload through standardized and flexible processes, capability demand management, and a holistic enterprise mindset.

Compelling, indeed, but without elaboration it is too abstract. Leadership will have a heavy hand in the top-level vision of the future, but it will be up to the team to do the legwork needed to elaborate it further. It is enriched with tiers of detail, describing what the future enterprise actually will do, with as much specificity as possible. Building on the statement, the architecting team creates a next level of detail for the envisioned future that adds more clarity and definitions. This should also provide a clear picture that motivates the transformation and drives future action. For example:

• Human resource accounting is accurate and transparent, providing decision makers with insight into distribution of people and authorizations.

- Program status is current and available, allowing resource managers to plan more effectively and anticipate dynamic changes in requirements.
- Resource management processes are consistent and documented across the functional areas of the enterprise, and supported by directors and senior executives throughout the enterprise.
- Program resources are fully traceable to an integrated master schedule, with resource loading mapped to the lifecycle phase.
- Resource requirements prioritization is data-driven and incorporates program priority, lifecycle phase, program impact, and portfolio impact.
- New hire requirements are filled within an average of four weeks once approved by the relevant business unit executive.

The detail gives a better picture of the envisioned future. Ideally, these statements represent the perspective of multiple enterprise constituents and key stakeholders. Still, they feel very passive.

Story of the Future

A further way to make the envisioned future come alive is with the technique of stories. It is often the case that the first attempt at an elaborated vision will be "dry," yet it needs to motivate people. It is certainly possible to create an envisioned future that motivates. The form of a newspaper article appearing years in the future reporting on the results of the transformation is one effective way, as illustrated below:

Smart City No Longer a Dream

October 24, 2019. The city management model has been radically transformed during the last five years through a transformation designed and led by Rosa Services. Public services, such as waste collection, street cleaning, energy efficiency and public lighting are now delivered in a more effective and efficient way, providing citizens with the opportunity to be involved in the service delivery, by participating in crowd-sourcing initiatives as well as intelligent platforms for the cities. Rosa Services is probably the most successful case study in this field. The company has developed a framework to measure their performance through outputs and measurable benefits for the citizens. The services integration has resulted in cost savings of more than 15% and more flexibility for the services delivery. Their open ecosystem and partnerships with leading academic institutions has provided them with the opportunity to bring open innovation to the cities. Thanks to Rosa Services we can now say that the Smart City is not just a dream, it is a reality. (National Press)

Imagining the impact of the transformation, at the end of the time horizon, is a great way to motivate buy-in. This news story speaks to all of the enterprise's stakeholders, including the general public as an audience. Another technique is to tell stories of personal impact. Not only are these powerful for buy-in, but they also provide a means to test the vision in regard to stakeholder value delivery. We refer to these personal stories as *vignettes*.

Creating Vivid Vignettes

We have found that formulating vignettes that portray how the envisioned future might be operationalized—that is, what the enterprise looks like when it has become a reality—can be a powerful tool for sharing the future vision at the personal level. Vignettes help to humanize the transformation by showing how stakeholders contribute to and benefit from the transformation strategies. A vignette can be limited to a single stakeholder, but it may be more powerful when developed for a small set of key stakeholders, because we can see the impact of the transformation through the eyes of each of these constituents. We now look at an example case.

For the first five decades of its existence, WP Guidance Corporation (WPGC) made highly specialized guidance systems for small commercial planes.[1] Then, in 2005, the firm undertook a major transformation to take advantage of an opening in the market for military flight guidance systems. The objective was to become a world-class leader in providing state-of-the-art flight guidance systems based on a set of unique algorithms invented by WPGC engineers, and to parlay that leadership into the market for large commercial jets as well. The WPGC architecting team created several vignettes to describe the company after its transformation, circa 2010.

The first vignette describes the envisioned posttransformation enterprise through the eyes of the customer:

Today, WPGC customers at Boeing, Airbus, and in the military realm, too, are fully confident that our guidance systems provide the full operational capability they need to ensure the best possible performance of their aircraft. Our customers consistently receive their equipment on time, built completely to their specified requirements. The systems are easy for pilots to learn and operate. Maintenance time and costs are well below the industry standard for other guidance systems. Whether used for military operations in the air or transporting passengers and cargo, the aircraft with WPGC systems have a decisive edge over the competition. How did WPGC get there? Any customer who has dealt with us for more than a decade will tell you that dealing with WPGC is like a new experience. There are no longer any silos. Organizational boundaries that previously tended to get in the way of innovation have disappeared. Each part of the WPGC enterprise is recognizably different. Cycle times are shorter, and customers notice. Training is less time-consuming and far less expensive. The systems work from the get-go.

The second vignette comes from the WPGC leadership perspective. Imagine the CEO giving a speech at the stockholders' meeting, reporting on the company's transformation:

Today, WPGC is recognized throughout the industry for the strength of its leaders in both the military and commercial sectors of its business. In fact, the cultivation of leaders at WPGC has become a topic of some discussion in the business press. The company is increasingly touted for its careful attention to career assignments, management training, and job-sharing experiences across the enterprise. In a recent article in the *Wall Street Journal*, WPGC was featured prominently in an assessment of how companies align their performance metrics with their overall enterprise objectives.

One reporter for *Fortune* magazine, noting the fast ascent of WPGC compared to competitors, made specific mention of what she called the "WPGC approach to talent pool management." This approach has greatly increased the company's ability to grow leaders across the enterprise. "WPGC seems to have made great strides," she wrote, "in aligning levels of work with levels of responsibility and position. People who come to work not only know what to do, but they have a clear sense of where they themselves are going in the company.

When you do what *Fortune* described, it's easy to reap big benefits. Today's WPGC leaders are forward looking, have a long-term enterprise view, and enjoy great incentives to do what is best for WPGC.

In a third vignette, we imagine the future enterprise through the eyes of the executive responsible for enterprise processes and practices:

We have met our objective by implementing an integrated business model enabled by streamlined and standardized processes that affords access for WPGC employees, the WPGC leadership, and other key stakeholders to timely, accurate, and usable products and information. This makes it possible to understand, assess, and guide the enterprise very quickly, creating a level of lifecycle management that once could only be imagined. Development and support costs have decreased by 35 percent. Time to market is a third of what it once was. Success has become routine.

In a fourth vignette, we hear more about the internal landscape of the enterprise, this time from the chief information officer's perspective:

It used to take weeks to get some of the information WPGC people needed to do their jobs. Today, information flows through the entire enterprise in hours, and often instantaneously. Paper is virtually nonexistent; electronic data movement is the norm. Everything moves seamlessly in parallel, and thanks to the great advances in blowing up the old silo structure and developing compatible exchange standards, the kinds of information blockages and inefficiencies we used to experience are a distant, bad memory. Now, appropriate information flows between administrative, engineering, and manufacturing departments as well as to and from customers and suppliers. The information incompatibilities and delays simply no longer exist.

Clearly the vignettes tell a more compelling story than a simple bulleted list of envisioned outcomes of the posttransformation enterprise would. Remember, as you read these, none of this has actually happened yet. The question is "How can these stories become the reality?" Our experience is that this approach enriches the thinking in the visioning activity, and the resulting vignettes are more powerful in motivating leadership and staff to engage in the transformation by using these as communication tools.

Stakeholder-Based Vignettes

Let us look at one more example of using vignettes for future-state elaboration through stakeholder perspectives, this time for a retiree healthcare system (the case we discuss in chapter 4), addressing the issue of living in multiple geographic regions during the course of a year. At the highest level, the vision can be stated as "Traveling retirees receive quality, timely care from the healthcare system regardless of where they are in the network."

While a simple statement of this sort captures the essence of the future, it is only the beginning. Next, the architecting team set out to describe, more fully, what the enterprise would look like approximately five years out:

Five years from now, referral managers are at the center of the enterprise. They coordinate care for retirees traveling away from their home providers and work closely with other key stakeholder groups, especially primary-care providers and primary-care managers. Stakeholders from all relevant groups are actively engaged in suggesting process improvements and are helping implement these improvements. There is an active education process that creates a wider knowledge base on the integrated nature of providing care for traveling retirees.

Next, the architecting team created a vignette to describe how it all works from the perspective of a healthcare recipient. In the present enterprise, traveling clients find it an ordeal to receive care outside their home region. The regional care systems are not well connected, and getting authorization for treatment is often confusing. Insurance claims out of the patient's home region can take months to resolve. Imagine how pleased the client would be in the envisioned future situation the following vignette describes:

Stephen Brooks is a 67-year-old retiree who resides in Boston, Massachusetts. He completed treatment for skin cancer last year, and while the cancer is in remission, he requires ongoing, coordinated care. When in Boston, he is treated by a physician in our Northeast regional care provider network (NeNet), but he is a "snowbird" and spends five months of each year in Florida, which is geographically part of the Southeast regional care provider network (SeNet).

Mr. Brooks's case is coordinated jointly by referral case managers in both NeNet and SeNet, and he is assigned to a Traveling Care Provider (TCP) within SeNet for the period when he is in Florida. His medical records, for which NeNet is responsible, are completely visible within SeNet. His primary-care provider in NeNet transmits care plan information to the two regional care managers and the TCP automatically and seamlessly.

Prior to Mr. Brooks's annual arrival in Florida, he already has set up an appointment with his SeNet-based TCP. On the appointment day, he simply shows up at the TCP's clinic; other than getting through the introductions, the TCP has everything needed to treat him. Subsequent appointments are scheduled, and when he is ready to return to Boston the medical records are sent back to his NeNet Primary Care Provider (PCP) for review. Of course, if there is any need for consultation between the PCP and TCP in the interim, this happens* without any bureaucratic delay.

How, then, will the enterprise make this happen? From a leadership insider, this vignette discusses how this will have been operationalized:

New systems and processes enable all this. The enterprise now has an entire TCP construct established, and robust coordination among regional care managers has become an everyday occurrence. Managers, care providers, caseworkers, and administrative staff completed extensive training on the streamlined processes some time ago, including how to use the enhanced metrics system that tracks traveling patients, both to feed information into the general data pool and also to maximize the efficiency and effectiveness of their local work.

Creating the envisioned future of the enterprise takes time and effort. This is not a simple exercise, but rather necessitates deep discussions with multiple stakeholders. Architects need to get at the essence of what each major stakeholder envisions. What do they see that changes the enterprise for the better? What needs to be added and enhanced? What do they hope may go away? The closer the team can get to encapsulating what each stakeholder envisions along with issues identified in the current-state analysis that need to be improved, the easier it will be to create alternative architectures that match the stakeholder's desires. The vision is important, but it is the visioning process that adds the most value. It enriches the thinking around possibilities and gains buy-in of stakeholders for where the enterprise hopes to be in the future. Vignettes make the vision for the future come alive.

Element-Based Narrative

One additional technique we find effective for envisioning the future is to write a more comprehensive narrative than the short news article that appears in the press at the end of a transformation. An elaborated version emulates the write-up for the annual report to be published in the year the transformation is completed. The enterprise elements are used to frame the story, as we illustrate in the following case.

Acme Transport is an enterprise that is a newer business unit of a large established automotive firm.[2] The unit wants to evolve to be a premier design unit in the larger corporation. The transformation starts in the year 2012 and was planned for a five-year horizon. Below is the excerpt from an envisioned annual report, developed using the enterprise elements to organize the narrative.

Strategy

Over the past several years, Acme Transport has presented itself as one of the premier and most efficient design arms of Global Transportation Corporation. This level of excellence was a result of years of implementing a new strategy that focuses on people and execution excellence while maintaining a high sense of urgency. This innovative strategy helped reduce the production cost of cars while maintaining Acme Transport's high standards. One of the important pillars of the strategy is synergy between employees and management that fosters a culture of high performance capable of tackling and solving new challenges. The strategy was a success because everyone in the division knew their role and brought unique skills and capabilities to the job, which allowed Acme Transport to create a balance in specialties and integration capabilities.

Product/Service

Last month, Acme Transport successfully launched the first car model fully designed within the business unit. The success for the unit is the result of a strategy the branch adopted in 2010. The new vehicle is expected to set a new bar for cars in its class in regard to price, features, and quality. During the design of the car, Acme Transport successfully managed to save 17% compared to the prior model of the car. At the same time, the new car is equipped with the latest technological features and has an expandable platform that will allow incorporating future features. The car will be available in the market as early as the third quarter of 2015, four months before its planned release date. The success in managing the project's three areas (cost, quality, and time) is a testament to the capabilities of Acme Transport.

Process

Today Acme Transport is proud to say that their engineering team has evolved into a process-centric organization. In alignment with the One Acme Transport initiative, they have standardized work to reduce costs and deliver consistently high-quality products. The teams all follow the standards established by the global engineering team and they have improved those processes in areas where they saw room for improvement. In addition to adherence to global processes, they have documented local processes to capture the way they work. Standard work is used as a means of knowledge transfer. Improved training processes support their commitment to these standards so that everyone benefits from the collective knowledge they have acquired and the best practices they have identified. As a result, their quality rating is the highest among all division engineering teams across Acme Transport. Also, new-employee surveys and assessments show excellent understanding of the process.

Organization

Four years ago the organization of Acme Transport was not enabling the enterprise to achieve its objectives. The organization was based on a model originally developed for operation in the home office geographic area. The matrix organization requires reporting to a functional manager and a program manager, with no real benefits coming from the organization. Additionally, many positions were duplicated in both locations, which was a waste of resources. Another problem was that the employee-to-supervisor ratio was too high. This affected the entire organization because employees did not feel they received the support they needed. Acme Transport has addressed each of these issues. The matrix organization has been reworked to create more value. The organization has been streamlined to eliminate duplicate roles. Resources are located with the teams they work with, which has made the design teams much more flexible and nimble. Supervisors were hired and employees now have the necessary support. This is evident in the results of employee surveys and the top-notch performance that allows Acme Transport to deliver vehicles consistently ahead of schedule.

Knowledge

Acme Transport used to be a "new" and "young" organization, and knowledge in its employees was insufficient. The division created a target for the breakdown of experts, experienced engineers, and new engineers required in a high-performance design team based on previous experience within Acme Transport. Plans were created to help employees develop the necessary skills and achieve the desired knowledge base. Employee capabilities were determined based on self-assessments but verified by supervisors and coworkers. This allowed individuals to recognize skills they needed and to develop training plans aligned with company vision.

Infrastructure

Acme Transport has demonstrated their commitment to the environment through infrastructure investments. Facilities and policies are environmentally friendly and have reduced costs. Some of the highlights of this effort include: (1) reduced power consumption by 10%; (2) reduced water consumption by 15%; (3) entirely paperless; and (4) 90% of all waste is recycled. They have also developed a social media environment to better connect employees across divisions. They facilitated initial face-to-face connection by sponsoring company parties, clubs, and sports leagues. Social media connections have increased by over 200%. The benefit has been observed in improved work interactions between the teams in the division. This effort has been a key to driving down development cycle times by 8%.

Information

Previously, information was not available for new hires to learn the processes including design rules and requirements. In response, Acme Transport has made a concerted effort to clarify all processes and create an online system that makes important processes easy to find and accessible to all employees that may need them. Design rules and engineering requirements have been clearly identified across areas through top-level processes. Training processes now familiarize employees with the processes and the way to find them. Each design team has taken responsibility for maintaining processes and ensuring their clarity to everyone on the team.

As can be seen in this example, using the view elements to describe the post-transformation enterprise helps to begin the identification of specific transformation objectives and actions that will need to be taken. Seeing the results in a "tell the world" format shapes thinking on what will have importance and impact. Architecting teams find that these types of exercises are instrumental in understanding the trajectory along multiple dimensions, and how unique changes contribute to the transformed enterprise as a whole. Often these visionary exercises are great ways to gather input from executive leaders and to communicate the future vision to various stakeholders. The results can become critical not only to the future enterprise design, but also as a platform to help motivate the transformation downstream.

Determining Evaluation Criteria

Before moving on to generating the alternative architectures, it is important to define the criteria that will be used to judge the goodness and fit of these architectures, in regard to realizing the vision for the future enterprise. Having an appropriate set of criteria is essential for making good architecture decisions. The criteria should be chosen in light of the major stakeholders and the capabilities the enterprise wants to possess in the future. A long-term view, to the extent possible, should be reflected in the criteria selected. The team needs to have a shared understanding of what all the criteria precisely mean, and often it is helpful to define subcriteria for this purpose. Leadership buy-in of the criteria is also essential. This must all be completed before moving on to the next step in the process, to avoid bringing bias into the evaluation.

Once there is clarity about the envisioned future and precise criteria for judging the possible architectures, our team can turn to the next activity, generating concepts capable of achieving the transformation vision.

Creating a Holistic Vision of the Future

Exercises to apply to your own enterprise

- Utilize the view elements and stakeholders to describe what your future enterprise aspires to be.
- Write a newspaper article five years into the future that tells the story of your envisioned enterprise.
- Formulate vignettes to depict the operationalization of the vision.

Questions for consideration

- Does your envisioned future statement tell a story that is compelling and will motivate change?
- Have your included your key view elements and eliminated silos?
- Are there clear indicators for success? Stretch goals?
- What will it be like to work in this new organization?
- What new ideas or concepts for future architectures are inspired by your envisioned future?

7 Generating Alternative Architectures

I would like my architecture to inspire people to use their own resources, to move into the future.

—Tadao Ando

The architecting process, thus far, has largely been about gathering information and insights. By now, the team has a good understanding of the enterprise landscape and how it could possibly change in the future. Stakeholder analysis is complete, and the current (as-is) enterprise architecture is captured. This, along with the holistic vision for the future, provides the knowledge to move forward. Now, the team is ready to begin its most creative task—generating ideas and discovering what architectures are possible.

Alternative architectures are the result of an iterative activity. This involves ideation, coming up with options, and using the options to inform the generation of several alternative architectures. The resulting alternatives are the contenders for the future architecture. The architects will spiral through these activities, while assessing the overall goodness and fit, and gather interim feedback. It is not really possible to say how many iterations it may take, and how many times the team might have to "go back to the drawing board." Ultimately, the activity ends with several viable alternative architectures, and the degree to which these are developed is often a function of the schedule for the project. It is always possible to continue ideation and concept creation, but practically speaking, time pressure will usually bring the activity to a close. In cases where the schedule is not the driver, the team will decide when there is "saturation." Saturation means the activity is producing neither significant new insights nor novel alternatives.

Ideation

Generating novel concepts begins with coming up with ideas for achieving the envisioned future of the enterprise. This activity is creative; there are no rules

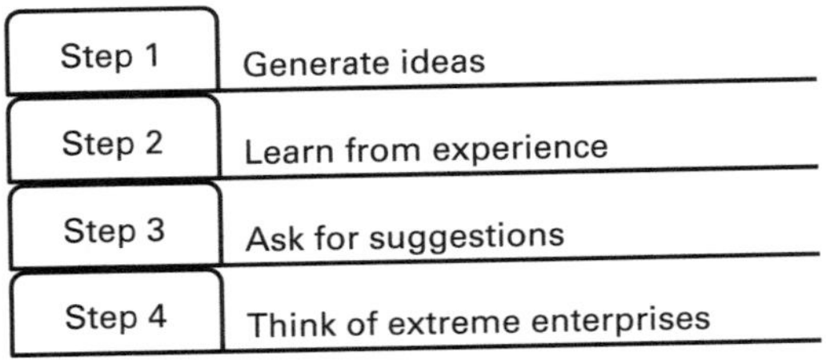

Step 1	Generate ideas
Step 2	Learn from experience
Step 3	Ask for suggestions
Step 4	Think of extreme enterprises

Figure 7.1
Four-step approach for ideation

to follow and openness to ideas of all kinds is important. The team needs to set aside limitations and ignore, for now, viability, cost, schedules, and other constraints. These are concerns for the next round. The goal of ideation and discovery is to generate a good number of concepts.

Moving beyond creating the vision for the future enterprise, one approach that has worked well is to come up with a large set of ideas. Figure 7.1 shows four activities useful in the ideation activity.[1] First, the team does its own generation of ideas. Second, it looks to experiences that other enterprises have had in similar situations. Third, the team can ask for suggestions both within and outside the enterprise. The final ideation activity in this approach is to look at extreme enterprises—that is, those that are either best in class or worst in class. By doing so, the team can gain insights on what has made these other enterprises highly successful or not, and whether the new architecture could adopt or avoid what these other enterprises have done.

We have found the use of typical creative brainstorming techniques works well to encourage an open and playful approach to the task at hand.[2] This is the time for out-of-the-box thinking, avoiding any tendency to let the realities of the enterprise landscape get in the way of idea generation. Of course, there will be a strong pull to be practical and realistic given the enterprise culture, resources, and time factors. For example, becoming a global market leader with 100,000 employees over a two-year period would appear unrealistic for a 20-person start-up enterprise. Yet this goal may only be unrealistic for the transformation time horizon and investment capital. Becoming the large global enterprise may, in fact, be exactly the path to take over a longer time horizon. This is why architecture alternatives are generated in the context of the time horizon for transformation.

Regardless, it is important to not let anything get in the way of coming up with interesting concepts during the initial discovery activity. Great ideas may be found in concepts that are simply not affordable or really cannot be

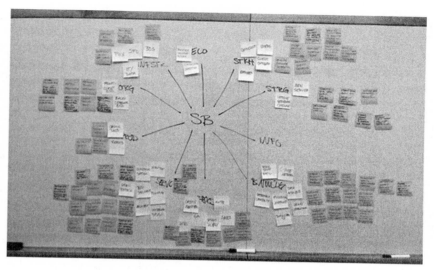

Figure 7.2
Discovery of attributes and grouping using view elements

implemented. The value of bringing such concepts into the decision process is that they may have interesting features that the team could end up giving serious consideration to. And there is value to be found in exploring what, precisely, makes a concept unrealistic.

There are many ways to go about the ideation process. One approach that we have seen work well for teams is to use sticky notes to capture desirable attributes of the future architecture, and then to group these attributes in some logical way, as shown in figure 7.2. In this example, the darker sticky notes record desired attributes that currently do not exist, and the lighter sticky notes highlight current attributes that architects want to retain in the new architecture. These notes are grouped in this case by the view elements (though other schemes to logically group the ideas are certainly possible).

Generating Novel Concepts

Once a set of desired attributes is generated, the architecting team uses this information to guide the creation of novel concepts. In this activity, themes start to emerge, and a set of architectural concepts is the result.

There is significant value in generating novel concepts before producing alternative architectures. It can be tempting to skip this activity with the pressures of time and urgency, and instead go directly to deriving more practical architecture alternatives. Generating concepts first allows more freedom to think creatively, building knowledge of what may or may not work in a future architecture without going into much detail. Jumping directly to the more "obvious" solutions saves time, but it is at the expense of failing to discover new possibilities. Some of the most far-reaching and impossible ideas can trigger a line of thinking that ends up leading to a practical innovation that might otherwise never have been conceived.

There are several guidelines for the art of concept generation. One is to stop worrying about whether a concept is "right." In fact, worrying about whether the concept is even feasible has no place in the ideation activity, although it makes sense to be reasonable. Here, architects should push back against those in the enterprise who insist "we can't do that." The activity is, however, not brainstorming with a completely blank canvas. The concepts are based on all the work that has come before in the architecting project. Insights can be gained through the perspectives of the eight view elements. In addition, considering pertinent soft factors such as trust or social responsibility or loyalty may also spark ideas.

A simple SWOT analysis is one effective way to identify the differentiating attributes of the concepts. Assessing concepts encourages deeper thinking about what is possible, and informs the next activity of formulation of *alternative architectures*. These are architectures that are viable, given where the enterprise is today and where it wants to be in the future. By viable, we mean they appear to have a reasonable chance of realizing the envisioned future, all things considered.

If the SWOT analysis suggests a concept is not viable, the team may discard the option, but not without asking whether there are strengths and opportunities in the concept that might be combined into a viable concept. There is no exact process for this; rather it requires some back-and-forth to get to a set of viable concepts for the next round. SWOT and similar tools provide a way to weed out architectural concepts that simply do not support the enterprise's vision for its future, or that are simply overwhelmed by weaknesses and threats to the degree that they are rendered infeasible or too risky to pursue.

It can be very useful to consider options that would take the enterprise to an extreme situation or in an extreme strategic direction. Many of the architecting teams we have worked with have arrived at some of their best ideas for concept architectures by thinking about best and worst cases. To be sure, the concepts at the extremes are not likely to be enacted, but there is real impact in simply giving them consideration.

Thinking about extremes fosters creative thinking because it forces the team to get out of its comfort zone. For example, what if the enterprise decided to close its office in a certain region that was also a major market? Analyzing this extreme option would help shed light on the real value of the regional office. What if an enterprise created an entirely new business model—for instance, changing from a for-profit enterprise with shareholders to a not-for-profit enterprise? Though such a transformation is highly unlikely, just thinking about it would bring up very interesting questions about the enterprise's core value proposition and business performance metrics. What if an enterprise outsourced all its engineering design? Considering such an extreme option could lead the architecting team to think deeply about the value of knowledge as an asset.

The activity of coming up with alternative concepts and thinking about their goodness and fit is, of necessity, more art than science. In his highly influential book on architecting organizations, Eberhardt Rechtin asserts that science is not enough because enterprises "by definition and from practical experience, are just too intricate and interconnected for realistic quantitative analyses."[3]

Down-Selection of Concepts

Once concepts are generated, a first round of down-selection serves to separate the "could be" options from the "couldn't be" and "shouldn't be" options. "Couldn't be" options are just not feasible under any reasonable circumstances, no matter how great the idea may be. Feasibility will mean different things for different enterprises. A "first come, first served" queuing process works for a bank or a fast food restaurant. A hospital that has been getting a lot of complaints about the waiting time in its emergency room couldn't possibly adopt a strategy to see patients in the order in which they arrive at the ER. Imagine the serious implications if life-threating injuries were not treated as a priority.

Typically, "shouldn't be" options are ones that turn out to be something other than what the architecting team is really after, and what the enterprise truly needs. These simply fail to satisfy the key strategic requirements for a future architecture. They looked good until the team delved deeper. Some "shouldn't be" options are easy to eliminate nearly from the start, but there is still benefit in putting them on the table for discussion. In one enterprise we studied, the team came up with a concept to support an aggressive expansion into a new region to satisfy a revenue growth goal. This seemed like a great option at first, but on further examination, the team realized the level of competition in that region diminished the profit potential they had initially envisioned. Naturally, this made the option much less attractive. In the end, it was decided this really should not be carried forward given many more promising options.

Eliminating "couldn't be" and "shouldn't be" concepts leaves the team with a set of "could be" concepts. If too few options are on the table, some additional idea generation may be wise. Our experience is that ideally, five to seven concepts may go forward to the next activity of generating alternative architectures. This appears to be just enough to keep it interesting but few enough to allow for effective comparison and reasoning.

Convergence of Concepts into Alternative Architectures

With a set of concepts in hand, the architecting team has the task of bringing these together toward the generation of several alternative architectures. These alternative architectures build on the concepts from the prior activity, but rather than simply taking the concepts and adding more detail, they are likely hybrids and extensions of these earlier ideas. Considering the strengths and shortfalls of each concept, the architecting team enriches the prior work through intentional combinations of various elements from positive features of the concepts. Multiple iterations may be needed depending on the available time, and whether new knowledge is still being uncovered. Often, an entirely new architecture can emerge through combinations of various features. This is perfectly natural, since the prior activity of concept generation was all about building knowledge of the possible.

Simple sketches facilitate the convergence of ideas into concepts. Sketches can be combined to create a storyboard. A storyboard, a sequence of sketches, is a powerful way to tell a story of how the future enterprise looks and behaves. Similarly, a series of concepts could be used to envision an incremental change involving two or more alternative architectures.

This is where asking what-if questions is essential. What if we outsource all manufacturing? Conversely, what if we bring more manufacturing inside to be closer to design engineering? What if we stop building our products and become assemblers and shippers, using commodity parts we can purchase from suppliers? Questions like these lead to the essential question: What will the future architecture look like under such circumstances? The architecting team may come up with options that directly challenge some existing policies and long-held cultural assumptions.

In one architecting project we studied, the team realized there were severe budget limitations. Those budget limitations were holding back the ideas and needed to be eliminated to allow the team to think beyond the current constraints. So, the team generated concepts without regard to cost, ignoring the budgetary constraints they may already have known were a reality. They did so not because they were capricious, but because they recognized that the very thing that might overcome budgetary constraints in the future architecture might be missed without this expanded thinking. Once the team had identified a set of potential architectures, they graded each one against pragmatic considerations such as affordability, which effectively filtered out infeasible solutions.

This approach may seem somewhat pointless—after all, why generate an architecture that will be filtered out at a later stage? However, that misses the point. There may be specific features of an infeasible architecture that can be applied to other feasible architectures. In other words, while a given architecture in its entirety may not be feasible, some features of that architecture may, in fact, be quite useful and desirable for the future state. Outside-the-box thinking at the beginning brings these sorts of features to light. The objective is to expand the boundaries to foster ingenuity and creativity, and thus widen the range of possibilities. As an example, the "first come, first served" approach would not work for the hospital emergency room as a whole (as we discussed earlier in this chapter). However, if the hospital applied a triage approach first, the patients put into the "minor-injury" category could be treated in this manner.

As architectural options are generated, the team is likely to raise specific ideas that may serve as drivers and enablers for later implementation. Perhaps doubling the research budget would be a key to expanding market share. Maybe a new leadership structure is seen as the key driver to achieving the vision for agility in service delivery. We observe a tendency on the part of architecting teams to let thinking too much about feasibility can get in the way of option generation. Would our risk-averse CEO support the doubling of the research budget? Do we have the right leaders to fit an envisioned new management structure? The team should keep a record of these implementation drivers and enablers to bring forward once a future architecture is decided on, and the implementation planning is taking place.

Possibilities generated and knowledge gained through the concept generation spiral provide the foundation of ideas. Just as they did in the as-is enterprise analysis, the elements again provide useful lenses for considering the whole enterprise. Here, though, we find that using a preferred order of elements for deriving architectures is helpful. This order has emerged from our work with numerous real-world enterprises.

Order for Considering the Elements

Our experience suggests four clusters of elements that, considered sequentially, provide a useful path for this architecting task (table 7.1). It is not a hard-and-fast rule because a particular situation might require another approach,

Table 7.1
Suggested order for considering elements

Iterative spirals through the sequence	Cluster sequence	Enterprise elements
	First cluster	Ecosystem Stakeholders
	Second cluster	Strategy Process Organization Knowledge
	Third cluster	Products Services
	Fourth cluster	Information Infrastructure

but for most cases this seems a natural progression of thinking about the elements.

The first cluster consists of the ecosystem and stakeholders; this is essentially our "canvas"—the backdrop for each of the architectures the team creates. Here, we are particularly interested in what is changing, or potentially could change. For example, is a new market emerging? Is there a policy on the horizon that will affect the product line? Do we anticipate there could be new stakeholders in the future? How will these issues impact our strategy?

The second cluster includes the strategy, process, organization, and knowledge elements, considered in that order. Strategy drives everything, and process (whether explicit or tacit) is how strategy is executed. Following process, we think about organization, and then knowledge that is required and generated. It is a sequence, but clearly one has to spiral through these to think about them holistically.

The third cluster consists of the products and services of the enterprise. This means considering what these are today, as well as the existing relationships of the products and services. And thought needs to be given to the products and services in the context of the envisioned future of the enterprise. What might be at risk? Where might there be opportunities?

The information and infrastructure elements comprise the fourth cluster. Given the other view elements, the information is what is needed to feed into and across the various elements. The infrastructure is what enables the operations of the enterprise, and what supports the products and services.

The team will spiral through thinking about all the elements, but it's really impossible to think of all ten elements as a whole. These four clusters seem to be natural groupings based on our experience, and the sequence of considering the clusters, and elements within the clusters, has proven to be a good approach. One very important thing to recognize is that a sequential order does not imply an order of importance of these elements. Rather, it is just an order for thinking through them that flows naturally. And while we say "sequence," there are, of course, feedback loops between the activities.

Generating alternative architectures takes concentrated time and effort, so the team needs to schedule solid blocks of time to work together. Active dialogue among the individuals on the team is essential. We advise against an approach where the team uses a divide-and-conquer strategy, assigning each team member to develop a single alternative. The synergy of ideas, the debate on alternatives, and building on the thoughts of other teammates appear to be essential ingredients for coming up with interesting architectural alternatives. This activity must be given adequate time and attention, even as the pressure of getting to the final choice of architecture is always present.

Alternative Architectures

The outcome of this step in the ARIES process is a defined set of alternative architectures. Various formats are useful for capturing the alternatives. Visual illustrations of different architectures under consideration are helpful for comparison and for communicating the basic ideas. Simplicity is important for these graphics to be useful, but behind a simple graphic is much more detail, including descriptions of the elements. We find the illustrations themselves can be powerful for conveying key differences in the architectures. Thus, these are useful artifacts for developing a detailed description that can be effective in communicating with involved stakeholders. Another alternative is to present key information in tabular form. Table 7.2 offers an example (with partial information) of an architectural design firm seeking to expand its business model through additional types of services. Four alternative architectures have been generated; they are described using the four dominant enterprise elements employed by the architecting team in this project. When such a table is expanded, it enables a useful comparison of the alternatives.

The choice of text-based, tabular, or graphic descriptions is made by the team based on how they feel communication would best be achieved. Of course, it is very common for teams to use more than one type of characterization for the alternative architectures. When the architecting team completes its final work, it is typical for a report to be written to capture the effort. Text-based descriptions provide a rich narrative and are almost always included in a report.

Table 7.2
Comparison of four alternative architectures for an architectural design firm seeking to expand

		Alternative architectures—consultancy focus		
	Facility redesign	Architecture flexibility	Human factors	Operational and organization design
Ecosystem	Traditional market	Traditional + industry firms	New markets	Traditional + new markets
Strategy	Healthcare and education sectors focus	Target industry firms and labs	Focus on high tech, retail, and manufacturing	Use external networks for new markets
Process	(Same)	Scenario planning and options evaluation	Research, development, prototyping	New business development
Services	Space planning and studies on utilization	Facilities planning and studies on demand	Service design and industrial design	Enterprise design and modeling

A recent architecting project in a healthcare enterprise provides a nice example of narrative architectural descriptions.

Collaboration for Wellness Center (CWC) Case

We now look at the case of a top hospital that implemented a state-of-the-art facility called the Collaboration for Wellness Center (CWC) as an alternative to traditional care.[4] The mission of CWC is "Collaborative engagement of patients and care providers in the partnership for sustained health and wellness." At the time of this architecting effort, CWC was considered a pilot program serving the hospital employees only, and the hospital wished to expand the program to include a more diverse set of patients. The architecting team working on this project captured the current-state architecture of CWC starting with analysis of the enterprise landscape (internal and external), followed by extensive interviews and discussions with stakeholders. Areas flagged for improvement included lack of formal roles and responsibilities, undocumented best practices, lack of formal knowledge-sharing processes, and lack of metrics to incentivize continuous improvement. A detailed analysis of the current architecture by view element informed the concept generation activity, and the organization and knowledge views were determined to be dominant in regard to improvement opportunities. Overall, the environment provided by CWC was excellent and there was significant impetus toward expansion. A concern was that this fast growth needed to be very carefully managed to ensure continued success.

Following an activity to create a holistic vision of the future, the architecting team explored concepts and then generated four alternative architectures. We now take a closer look at these architectures, and how the team described them through examining the strengths, weaknesses, opportunities, and threats.

Architecture Option 1: Growth through Replication ("Copy Exactly")

CWC is currently working on future plans to serve more patients. The current strategy is to expand from one care team to three. Under this approach, this architecture leverages the "copy exactly" method used in a number of large manufacturing enterprises. With this method, CWC would replicate the care team along with the necessary processes and infrastructure required to operate independently.

Strengths and Weaknesses

Since the current care team is well-rated in terms of patient care, replication of the care team would help ensure that CWC is able to maintain the same high-quality care. "Copy exactly" assumes repeatable processes and an infrastructure of good documentation and best practices. Unfortunately, knowledge sharing, process documentation, and defined roles and responsibilities are weak points for CWC. These weak points are major barriers to successful replication through "copy exactly." Since the care team members do not have defined roles and responsibilities, it will be difficult to replicate how each staff member allocates his or her time per day. Many staff members have increased responsibilities outside their core competency. For example, the registered nurse-practitioner (RNP) performs normal nursing tasks, as well as many administrative tasks. The RNP administrative tasks would actually not go away but just increase in magnitude with additional teams. Without process documentation for these tasks, the RNP's duties will be hard to replicate. Additionally, the "copy exactly" approach assumes the "product" environment does not vary. This means that CWC would not be able to have each care team specialize in a certain population. For example, one care team could focus on heart disease prevention while the other team focuses on diabetes.

Opportunities and Threats

With accountable-care organizations (ACOs) at the forefront of healthcare discussions in the United States, CWC could find opportunities for growth if their current model is successful. If this model is repeatable and low cost, the government and other healthcare providers will want to copy it. This will bring opportunities to expand and possibly bring revenue to CWC. Conversely, a majority of employees in the hospital CWC is associated with may want to stay with their current providers, which would inhibit CWC's growth. Further, the CWC model has been implemented only with a health-conscious population of workers at the hospital. Based on data from the IMS Institute for Healthcare Informatics, the top 5 percent of the patients receiving care make up the top 50 percent of cost. At this current stage, CWC is not treating a group representative of the U.S. population.

Architecture Option 2: Growth through Additional Services in the Current Facility

Another avenue for growth at CWC is to add additional services at their current facility to encourage enrollment. This approach would transform CWC into a primary-care and wellness center that provides vertical healthcare services such as preventive care, health education, or early diagnosis like obesity counseling, mental health services, or physical therapy. Along with these verticals, CWC could expand into some specialist services such as radiology. With more services, employees may have further incentives to enroll with CWC, which in turn will justify expansion to three care teams.

Strengths and Weaknesses

By expanding into these vertical services and some specialist services, CWC will have a greater impact on cost reduction. These vertical services enhance CWC's preventive-care capabilities and will have a greater impact on their patient population. Further, by avoiding referrals to specialists, the hospital's claim payments will be reduced. Regarding weaknesses, additional services will add complexity to CWC's operations and likely increase coordination costs. Some services would require extra personnel or equipment that would further lower the enterprise's utilization of assets.

Opportunities and Threats

New technologies, such as handheld ultrasound devices, are becoming available to healthcare providers. These simple versions of medical devices make it easier to integrate new services into CWC's primary-care model. CWC could identify technologies that allow them to provide services without major capital investment. New personnel and equipment to expand services might be constrained by the size of CWC's facility. The size of the facility will likely restrict the types of services feasible there.

Architecture Option 3: Growth through Expansion to Other Customer Segments

Although providing services to nonhospital employees is not a part of the enterprise's current strategy, CWC could increase enrollment numbers if necessary by providing care to other members of the larger healthcare network to which it belongs. This network is interested in learning accountable-care best practices, which might incentivize them to allow CWC to expand their care model to surrounding providers in the regional area that serve different patient demographics. CWC could open their current center to other customer segments or begin setting up satellite clinics in the area.

Strengths and Weaknesses

This approach would stress-test CWC's patient-care model in different ecosystems. With access to a larger patient population, the care model could be tested with different patient populations. While expansion to other customer segments is great for learning, satellite centers would require a large fixed-cost investment. If the enrollment of the healthcare network employees was influenced by the location of CWC's office, satellite centers might be required to expand into new customer segments. This cost increase would hurt CWC's current utilization goals.

Opportunities and Threats

By collaborating with other healthcare providers, CWC could strengthen their care model through collaboration across the city. This allows for best practices to be shared and patient care to be improved. On the other hand, this approach has the threat that patients in certain demographics might not have access to virtual care to facilitate the continuous-care model. Because CWC's future continuous-care model is based on virtual care (i.e., Internet video conferencing), patients without such technology would be at a disadvantage in receiving the best care.

Architecture Option 4: Growth through More Virtual-Care Encounters

In this architecture, CWC would aggressively invest in IT infrastructure to increase virtual encounters relative to patient visits, thus allowing care teams to take a larger patient population without adding resources. This aligns with the strategy of CWC but risks decreasing the quality of patient care.

Strengths and Weaknesses

Accountable care heavily focuses on cost per clinical outcome and population management. The majority of the cost comes from patient visits and usage of equipment and resources. At times, short visits can be replaced by virtual care to minimize the claims and resource usage associated with patient visits. By addressing minor issues via virtual care, the overall cost per clinical outcome is reduced. The downside of increasing capacity through more virtual-care encounters is that it could lead to a reduction in the quality of patient care. For example, if a doctor misdiagnoses a condition virtually, the patient's condition could obviously worsen. Further, virtual care could result in an unsatisfactory work environment for doctors, nurses, and staff, where there is little face time with the patient.

Opportunities and Threats

CWC will be leveraging and leading a trend toward accessibility and consolidation of patient information in the Cloud. By investing in IT infrastructure and integrating that infrastructure with proven accountable-care organization processes, CWC could license its technology to other accountable-care organizations and create a new revenue stream for the hospital. The largest risk of virtual care is that liabilities could increase due to misdiagnosis or noncompliance with the laws that protect patient confidentiality.

Using this narrative approach works to describe the architectures and to see the merits of each. As with this case, it is easy to see that the "best" architecture is not easily revealed. The architects will need to perform trade-offs and weigh different choices.

Moving on to Evaluation

The process of generating alternatives may vary based on preferences of the enterprise, time available for the activity, and level of detail the team desires at this point in the process. We find that most architecting teams settle on three to five alternative architectures to undergo evaluation. This seems a reasonable compromise given limits on how many things humans can cognitively compare at once. We suggest that any more than five alternatives may diminish the chances of effectively evaluating these.

The attractiveness of any architecture can ultimately be judged in regard to the degree to which it can inspire others to invest time and resources to achieve it. In the end, the selected architecture must be compelling enough to motivate stakeholders who will be part of its implementation. Each of the alternatives resulting from this step in the process is considered in light of how it might perform given the challenges and circumstances envisioned in the future of the enterprise. We discuss evaluation in chapter 8.

Generating Alternative Architectures

Exercises to apply to your own enterprise

- Hold a session to come up with initial ideas.
- Generate seven to ten concepts and down-select to five.
- Use the concepts to generate several alternative architectures, considering the view elements in sequence (table 7.1).
- Prepare a comparison of these alternative architectures and their view elements as shown in table 7.2.

Questions for consideration

- Has the team used multiple ideation techniques to come up with ideas (see figure 7.1)?
- Were qualitative techniques (e.g., SWOT) used to assess and down-select to five to seven concepts?
- Did the team elaborate the alternatives using the enterprise elements?
- Are alternative architectures viable for achieving the envisioned future?
- Did the team record assumptions and concerns raised during the activity?

8 Deciding on the Future Architecture

If architecture had nothing to do with art, it would be astonishingly easy to build houses, but the architect's task—his most difficult task—is always that of selecting.
—Arne Jacobsen

Every architect faces the difficult question of when the work of designing architectures is complete. It is not unlike the artist who must decide when a painting is finished. There always seems to be more that could be added or changed. Throughout the design activity features of the candidate architectures were selected, and then perhaps moved around, modified, or even taken away. Architectures may have been deconstructed and recombined into new ones. Optimally, the design activity results in three to five candidate architectures to consider, each exhibiting the potential for performing well in the envisioned future for the enterprise.

At some point, the team needs to "draw a line in the sand" and move on to a formal evaluation of the candidate architectures and the selection of the future architecture. It is not an exact science, but neither is it entirely an artistic choice. Our architecting team will use specific criteria and a chosen evaluation method to make their decision.

Evaluation Criteria

Evaluation is about judging the goodness and fitness of the possible architectures based on a specified set of criteria. Throughout the time the team spends in the design of the candidate architectures, there is surely some informal evaluation taking place. Care must be taken, though, to avoid bias and keep an open mind. Earlier in chapter 6, we discussed the importance of deciding on an evaluation method and criteria prior to generating architectural concepts.

Careful consideration of what criteria are to be used for the evaluation is necessary early in the process to understand any inherent biases and minimize their effect on objective decisions. The selected criteria need to address a longer-term perspective to the extent possible, and take into consideration varied stakeholder needs. And, of course, leadership must fully buy into these criteria, which will drive the decisions for the future of the enterprise.

Fundamental to a good evaluation outcome, the team needs to be on the same page in regard to the basis for comparing alternative architectures. This necessitates a precise understanding of the evaluation criteria. For example, if scalability of the enterprise is one of the evaluation criteria, all team members need to interpret *scalability* the same way. What if one team member thinks scalability has to do with the ability to increase or decrease the size of the workforce, whereas another thinks it has to do with increasing or decreasing product manufacturing output. Perhaps the team discussed both at one point in time, but team members no longer remember how the discussions concluded. Clearly, such ambiguity in the evaluation criteria is going to have a major impact on architecture decisions. It is not enough to say scalability of the enterprise is a determinant; rather it must be more precise. Is it a scalable workforce, scalable business model, or scalable manufacturing facility? Each means something different.

The evaluation criteria take shape earlier in the architecting process as the team moves from envisioning the future to concept generation. It is best to avoid selection of criteria after the fact, because these may be suggested by choices in the architecture candidates. Of course, it is likely that some time will have passed since the criteria were first formulated. Since that time, initial concepts will have been generated and candidate architectures derived. Naturally, the team's thinking evolves, and changes may have taken place. Perhaps shifts in the ecosystem put new demands on the enterprise, such as an increase in competitors or a shortfall of suppliers. Perhaps there was a change in a critical stakeholder, who sees the world a bit differently than their predecessor. While we don't want to significantly alter the criteria originally selected, it is important to reaffirm the appropriateness of the criteria prior to beginning evaluation of possible architectures. Carefully thought out small adjustments could be necessary. For instance, an unexpected disruption in economic conditions in the ecosystem may increase the relative importance of affordability. When adjustments are made, or criteria are added or taken away, the team needs to be sure it understands if and where biases may be introduced.

Who Evaluates the Architectures?

Most likely the architecting team members will all be involved in the evaluation process, though it is certainly not required. For example, if too many individuals come from the same functional area of the enterprise, the team may elect to have one individual represent their group in the evaluation. It is important to ask the question "Who else should be involved in evaluating the alternative architectures?"

Earlier we discussed the importance of having a team that reflects the diversity of the stakeholders impacted by the transformation. At this stage it is equally—if not more—important to have equity in representation. If there is an unrepresented stakeholder group given the makeup of the team, it will be wise to recruit an evaluator who can speak for those interests. Additionally, the sponsor (or a designee) may sometimes directly participate in evaluation activities. When this situation arises, the team needs to take care to avoid being overly influenced by the sponsor's voice. Striving for a balance of perspectives is important.

Our studies have found that a highly desirable practice is to have a "nonadvocate" member on the evaluation team. Often team members and closely affiliated stakeholders are too entrenched in the organization to be able to take a fully unbiased view. A nonadvocate is someone who understands the enterprise and goals of the transformation, but will not be directly affected by this particular transformation. This individual could come from a noninvolved part of the enterprise. Or, the nonadvocate might be an outsider, perhaps a trusted supplier or partner, or an experienced consultant.

Future Proofing

The evaluation task involves making the difficult decision of which of the architectures under consideration is the best choice. Clearly, it makes no sense to choose an architecture fit only for the present, though it is only natural to think this way. The architecture needs to be suited to the targeted time horizon, and for the anticipated needs for the foreseeable future.

But we know the future does not always unfold as one might expect. The question, then, is how to select an architecture that will be robust and/or amenable to change over time. We can't predict the future, so the only thing we can practically do is some thoughtful testing to evaluate the architectures by considering alternative futures. How, then, can we decide which architecture has the best chance of being *future-proof*? Two useful techniques for evaluating architectures on their fitness for the future are testing at the extremes and scenario-based testing.

Testing at the Extremes

The first future-proofing technique, *testing at the extremes*, is about imagining extreme conditions (best and worst) the enterprise could feasibly encounter, even if the team believes these are almost inconceivable. Testing at the extremes involves thinking about how each of the candidate architectures would hold up under the best and worst cases. Recall that we used a similar approach in generating ideas. Here we think more specifically about the performance of each of the architectures under consideration, and how one compares to another.

As an example, suppose a commercial product company holds 30 percent of the market share in its industry, and the transformation goal is to expand from selling products to selling both products and services. While putting in place a new architecture to add services to the company's offerings, the leadership envisions retaining the 2 percent annual market share increase it has achieved in recent years.

Now, imagine the extremes. Maybe the worst imaginable case (while staying in business) is that market share decreases 5 percent per year, and the best that leadership could see happening is that market share increases by 15 percent per year. Given these imagined best- and worst-case market share outcomes, we ask how each of the candidate architectures would perform under such conditions. With the 5 percent decrease in market share, the enterprise might need to shut down 30 percent of its business units. While enterprises do sometimes consider "worst-case scenarios" in planning, we seldom see "best-case scenarios" given thoughtful consideration. A best case, while it may seem positive, can actually be problematic if the enterprise cannot effectively handle all the consequences.

Imagine, now, what the impacts of a 15 percent annual increase could be. The enterprise might need to double the number of business units to meet demand. This may actually be a difficult thing to practically achieve without a viable strategy in mind. Perhaps, as part of a new strategy, the enterprise could institute a preferred supplier program, where suppliers have already been vetted and business agreements are in place to enable rapid reaction when needs arise. Or, new facilities can be designed with excess physical space in case manufacturing needs to expand. It would be important to plan for these contingencies in advance.

Testing at the extremes can be done with a best-worst pair to consider single factors, such as market share. One can also imagine a set of best-worst conditions, woven together into scenarios for testing the candidate architectures under extreme circumstances. For example, a scenario might involve not only market share, but also economic conditions, supplier availability, and policy changes. What if economic conditions were so favorable that an available component supplier could not be found in the time window necessary for timely product release? What if a policy change suddenly prohibited doing business in one of the company's major geographic markets? Testing at the extremes can be a time-independent technique—that is, attention is on an alternative set of conditions rather than on when these conditions specifically occur.

Scenario-Based Testing

Scenario-based testing involves examining how each alternative architecture might perform under different imagined futures. This may or may not incorporate the time dimension, where scenarios occur in an order rather than one at a time.

Testing scenarios are "constructed" by considering which factors in the ecosystem appear most uncertain. These may have to do with economic conditions, market conditions, availability of technology, and other such factors. In addition to ecosystem factors, envisioned scenarios may be based on possible shifts in what stakeholders value. If fuel prices escalate dramatically, automotive market stakeholders are likely to show high preference for fuel economy over comfort and acceleration performance. As contrasted with the testing-at-the-extremes approach, here we envision more realistic scenarios—that is, those we think could quite easily happen in a changing world.[1] Ideally, the selected future architecture works in all of the scenarios tested, but more likely trade-offs will be needed.

Let's look at the case of how an architecting team working with Ivan Electronics Corporation (IEC), a U.S.-based manufacturer of personal electronics, evaluated the suitability of two candidate architectures using scenario-based testing.[2] Roughly 70 percent of IEC's product line is sold in the United States, with slow-growing demand in several other countries. While IEC manufactures most components used in its products, it does depend on two smaller companies to supply several components that are not cost-effective for IEC to produce itself. Presently, IEC outsources roughly 30 percent of its manufacturing to a company in India and 5 percent to a company in China.

The architecting team developed its testing scenarios by convening a meeting with IEC's functional-area leaders. During the meeting, the group elicited and discussed potential scenarios the enterprise could face within the next five years. Ideas for the scenarios were prompted through identifying a number of ecosystem uncertainties thought to be moderate to high. The uncertainty factors agreed on were costs related to labor, economic conditions in the United States, demand for IEC products outside the United States, and competitors in its market. Given a five-year time horizon, the group also projected a target for when the particular scenario would occur within the five-year horizon. Two scenarios are:

Table 8.1
Scenario-based testing of the two architectures for scenarios A and B

	Upside	Downside
Preferred Outsourcing Partners	Enables rapid change in location in which work is performed if labor prices escalate.	Increases likelihood and/or impact of outsourcing partner becoming competitor.
Wholly Owned Subsidiaries	Reduces likelihood and/or impact of outsourcing partner becoming competitor.	Economic-based issues more complex to deal with than changing outsourcing location.

Scenario A. In year 2, labor costs in India increase 30 percent due to new wage standards.

Scenario B. In year 4, two of IEC's outsourcing partners become major competitors.

Each scenario can be tested individually, or two or more can be considered in sequence. The objective is to discern what architectural features and strategies would enable IEC to be successful under the scenarios. Certain architectures are likely to perform well for a given scenario. For example, one of IEC's candidate architectures involved a strategy to identify ten or more preferred outsourcing partners in several countries that could be used as conditions demanded. Another candidate architecture involved establishing wholly owned subsidiaries in China, India, and Brazil instead of outsourcing to independent companies. Table 8.1 summarizes how these candidate architectures perform under scenarios A and B.

The "Preferred Outsourcing Partners" architecture could enable rapid change in the location where work was outsourced if labor costs skyrocket in India (scenario A), because IEC could quickly select a different outsource partner from its preferred list. The downside is that this architecture might increase the probability of outsourcing partners later becoming competitors (scenario B).

The "Wholly Owned Subsidiaries" architecture has the potential to reduce the likelihood or impact of outsourcing partners becoming competitors (scenario B). The downside of this architecture is that it may be more problematic under scenario A, since economic-based issues for an IEC subsidiary in India would be more complex to deal with than simply changing the location of where work is outsourced.

The purpose of testing at the extremes and scenario-based testing is not to select an "optimal" architecture. It is about exploring the strengths and vulnerabilities of the various architectures through the what-if dialogue fostered by these future-proofing techniques. This often prompts ideas for "tweaking" a candidate architecture. It is also possible that a new candidate architecture will be designed by combining features from the various potential architectures given new insights. Some degree of experimentation is involved, but this is at a deeper level than the playful approach we took in generating the early concepts.

Model-Based Evaluation

Depending on the complexity of the enterprise and the team's available time and resources, models can be used to evaluate specific aspects of the architecture. A deep discussion of model-based approaches is beyond the scope of this book, but we highlight a few important points. Since enterprises are complex and exist in a dynamic environment, it is rarely possible for a team to model the entirety of the enterprise for each of the candidate architectures under consideration. Such an effort would be time-consuming and resource intensive, and thus likely prohibitive unless the enterprise transformation was a complex, large-scope, and multiyear activity. Using models on more modest projects with shorter time-frames is possible and often very beneficial; the key is scoping.

Models are abstractions of the enterprise, so it is important to choose an approach that fits the facet of the architecture that needs to be most closely examined in the evaluation. Different types of models give insights in unique ways.[3] For example, *system dynamics* models[4] help to understand dynamic behaviors in an enterprise, while *process models* focus on process integration, workflows, and process performance. Such models can be implemented using computational approaches, and there are many useful software packages available. Models can also be "back-of-the-envelope," requiring little time but generating good insights. While limited and not taking advantage of computational power to quantify dynamic outcomes, simpler models can still build understanding.

Decision Methods

There are many approaches for deciding among alternatives, from simple to more complex methods and techniques. Many of these work well for group decision making, and so are suited for the architecting process. SWOT analysis and Pugh Concept Selection are techniques we find useful in comparing architecting concepts, as we discussed in chapter 7. The same techniques are well

Stakeholders	Criteria	Alternative architectures				
		Facility design consultants	Flexibility consultants	Human factors design consultants	Operations organization design consultants	Research and development
Employees, officers	Flexibility with human resources	0	0	0	0	0
Clients, officers	Flexibility with project customization	0	+1	+1	+1	0
Employees, officers	Compatibility with current competencies	+1	+1	0	0	−1
Officers	Adaptability of new competencies	0	+1	+1	+1	+1
Clients, officers	Affordability for firm and clients	+1	+1	−1	−1	0
Clients, officers	Replicability and reliability of services	+1	+1	+1	−1	0
Clients, officers	Long-term client relationships	0	+1	+1	+1	−1
Employees, principals	Innovatability	0	−1	+1	+1	+1
Employees	Draw for current and future culture	0	0	+1	+1	+1
	Total +1	3	6	6	5	3
	Total −1	0	1	1	2	2
	Total 0	6	2	2	2	4
	Total Score	3	5	5	3	1
	Overall implementability score	Easy	Easy/ moderate	Moderate/ difficult	Moderate	Moderate

Figure 8.1
Unweighted decision matrix

suited for architecture evaluation; we now look at how some of them were applied.

Figure 8.1 shows the *decision matrix* used for a transformation in Allan Design, an architectural design firm seeking to expand its current offerings. Nine criteria were decided on, and then mapped to the stakeholders who will place highest value on these criteria (as shown in the left column in the evaluation matrix in figure 8.1). The five alternative architectures under consideration were evaluated against the current-state architecture, as better (+1), worse (-1), or same (0), and summed to determine a total score.[5] The team then assigned a qualitative evaluation of the implementability from easy to difficult. As can be seen, there are two architectures that score "3" and two that score "5." Of the latter, the "flexibility consultants" architecture was determined to be easier to implement than the "human factors design consultants" architecture.

The Allan Design Group team chose to use nonweighted criteria, because they decided a simpler approach would be most effective for generating discussions, given the culture of the firm. Of course, it is rarely the case that all of the evaluation criteria are equally important. It is up to the team to bring these differences out in the discussions in making a final selection (this case is discussed further in appendix B).

A somewhat different evaluation approach was used by the architecting team on the ISSA project (this case is described in more detail in appendix A). The decision-making culture of ISSA, the software service group within a major corporation in the technology industry, is one where it is typical to use more

Criteria			Candidate architectures	As-is	Outsourcing all	Backsourcing	Outsourcing team	Process owner
Scalability	8%	Allows growth while minimizing complexity	50%	3	4	2	5	4
		Long-term relationshop and coordination	50%	2	5	5	5	4
Reliability	15%	Supplier excellence	75%	3	4	5	5	4
		Supplier availability	25%	4	4	5	5	4
Manageability	22%	Use of performance metrics	50%	2	4	5	4	3
		Facilitates communications	50%	2	3	3	4	3
Flexibility	9%	Ability to react to market conditions	100%	3	5	0	4	4
Cost	24%	Labor costs	40%	3	5	4	4	4
		Hidden costs	20%	4	2	0	3	3
		Implentation costs	40%	5	0	0	1	4
Cycle time	22%	Improves delivery compliance	65%	3	3	5	4	4
		Facilities lead-time reduction	35%	4	3	3	4	5
				3.1	3.41	2.86	3.89	3.81
		Ranking		4	3	5	1	2
		Risk and transformability		✔	✘	✘	★	✔

Figure 8.2
Weighted decision matrix

complex and quantitative techniques. On this project, instead of treating all criteria as equal, the team used weighted evaluation criteria.

A weighted decision matrix is easy to set up. Each evaluation criterion the team previously agreed on is assigned a percentage weight, summing to 100 percent. The ISSA team also felt the evaluation would be more effective if additional subcriteria were derived for each criterion. The subcriteria themselves are weighted, summing to 100 percent for each of the major criteria. In this architecting project, the subcriteria are short statements. The ISSA team arrived at the weighting using a discussion and consensus process. As a note, another effective approach is to pose the subcriteria as questions rather than statements.

Figure 8.2 shows the *weighted decision matrix*. There are six high-level criteria (scalability, reliability, etc.), each weighted and decomposed into subcriteria. For example, "reliability" is assigned a weight of 15 percent and decomposed into two lower-level subcriteria, "supplier excellence" subweighted at 75 percent and "supplier availability" subweighted at 25 percent (within the 15 percent weight for "reliability").

Rather than using a better-same-worse comparison approach, the ISSA team used an approach where the architectures, including the current (as-is) architecture, were assessed for effectiveness on a scale of 0 (worst) to 5 (best). Each member of the team assigned the effectiveness score individually, and then the team discussed and arrived at a consensus score for each criterion for the five architectures (the four candidates and the as-is architecture).

Using the consensus scores and weightings, a weighted average was computed, and then the team rank-ordered the architectures according to the computed averages. Separately, the team assessed each architecture on its implementation risk and transformability. This can be done in a quantified manner, or using a more qualitative approach. The ISSA team did the latter, assigning a stoplight color (green, yellow, or red). The evaluation team can then have a deeper discussion in regard to choosing a candidate architecture given all things considered—criteria, subcriteria, rankings, risk, and implementability. The completed decision matrix is then used to discuss the evaluation result with leadership, serving as a good visualization to support that discussion.

The architecting team will have gone through an intensive process and series of discussions in arriving at the selection of a future architecture. It can be a tough job to convey the compelling story behind why the architecture selected is the "right" choice. The decision matrix is one good artifact to share with the leadership and other stakeholders as this decision is revealed. This can also be augmented with other simple representations to help tell the story.

One representation we find quite effective to communicate the choice of architecture is a *radar plot*, sometimes called a *spider diagram*. This makes it visually simple to see how each candidate architecture scores in the evaluation criteria. Depending on the actual results, the radar plot may clearly show where one or more of the architectures are dominated by other candidate architectures, and where architectures are similar.

Showing simple evaluation results is useful, but there can be a risk that this will imply the decision was a simple one. In fact, there are many difficult trade-offs to be made. One of the significant trade-offs in choosing a future architecture relates to how much effort the enterprise is willing to expend to achieve a given level of effectiveness, and what risk it is willing to take.[6] There are various architecture trade-off methods that exist and have been used in enterprise architecting projects.[7]

The ISSA team found that this matrix facilitated having a productive discussion on the different alternatives with the top executives. Architecture A ("Strong Outsourcing") was quickly discarded as a feasible alternative because of its higher risk and implementation difficulties. Architectures B and C appeared to be equally effective, but B was deemed more risky than C and required more effort to implement. On the other hand, architecture D was less effective but easier to implement. It had, however, some scalability restrictions, making it more risky than architecture C.

Another visual we have found useful for making the evaluation results come alive, for the leadership and other stakeholders, is some form of scorecard. The scorecard is a simple one-slide summary that gives the viewer a snapshot of the evaluation scores and supporting information. The latter is often taken from a SWOT analysis, though there is no set format for a scorecard. The information contained in a scorecard is cogent.

Evaluation scorecards have proven effective in demonstrating that a deep evaluation of each candidate has been conducted, giving the key information needed for the architecting team to have a rich discussion with the stakeholders. A typical scorecard will include the name of the architecture, a brief description, results of scoring against criteria, and some additional information such as selected SWOT information. The scorecards illustrate the results of the evaluation, on an architecture-by-architecture basis. The scorecards can be placed side by side and easily compared since the information is conveyed in a common format. The scorecards tell the story of the decision itself.

Selecting the Future Architecture

When the analysis is sufficiently complete, or the schedule demands a decision be made with whatever information is available, it is time to make the selection. This is not as simple as just "turning the crank" and getting the decision. It is always going to involve expert judgment because there are always trades to be made.

As evaluation comes to an end, the team will need to capture the results for sharing with the sponsor and other stakeholders. It is challenging to portray the complex information developed over weeks or months, and especially to do so in a concise way. Several aspects must be communicated, including the overall architecture and benefits, the criteria used for evaluation, and how the selected architecture compares to other architectures considered. The techniques we have just discussed can be helpful, though there will also need to be more justification recorded. It is a good practice for an architecting team to write a formal architecture evaluation report, including the method applied in the evaluation, interim results, and the outcome of the evaluation.

Once the future architecture is decided, it is fairly certain that there will be remaining questions, uncertainties, and unknowns. In our next activity, the subject of chapter 9, most of these are resolved through the process of assessing alignment and making adjustments, and through specifying additional detail. Any remaining open concerns and issues will be captured in the implementation plan.

Deciding on the Future Architecture

Exercises to apply to your own enterprise

- Review your required enterprise capabilities defined earlier and assign weights for each one, giving consideration to specifying subcriteria.
- Evaluate your alternative architectures using the weighted capabilities as shown in figure 8.1.
- Examine both the risk and difficulty of implementation for each alternative architecture.
- Test your top architectures under different scenarios as illustrated in table 8.1.

Questions for consideration

- Have you obtained buy-in from your leadership sponsors on the capability ranking and evaluation methodology?
- Have you tested your alternative architectures at the "extremes" or under different future scenarios?
- What are the risk factors for your alternative architectures?
- What are the issues in transforming from the current state to the future architecture?

---

9 Developing the Implementation Plan

Failing to plan is planning to fail.
—Alan Lakein

With the future architecture now selected, the architecting team moves on to the final step in the ARIES process. The team's final deliverable is the new architecture, along with the plan for moving forward. This plan provides just enough detail to enable implementation without overconstraining the implementers.

Given the architecture describing "what" the future enterprise will be, the team needs to develop an implementation plan. This high-level plan focuses on the specific activities needed to move from the current state to the desired future state. It would be easy to start adding very specific implementation-related details to the plan, but the architect's role is to specify the necessary and sufficient detail for moving forward to the implementation phase. This plan serves as the basis for the next stage of transformation, involving detailed implementation planning and resourcing.

Assessing and Adjusting Alignment

A first activity in the planning step is to assess the alignment of strategic objectives, stakeholder values, key processes, and measures. While this was previously done for the current enterprise, now it is assessed for the future architecture in the context of the envisioned future of the enterprise. It is important to discover any gaps and weaknesses, and to make adjustments as needed before the implementation plan is set. Similarly, identifying the strong relationships is important so that the team can ensure these are retained and leveraged in the implementation effort.

Recall that in chapter 5 we use a technique called the X-matrix; this is useful once again now to assess the alignment for the future architecture. Any necessary adjustments to alignment within the architecture are addressed now, if possible.

The expectation is that there will be very few of these, but there may be a need to flag some things for further review when adding detail. Where there are gaps and weaknesses that need to be addressed in the future, these are identified with specific action to be taken as part of the implementation plan.

Suppose, for example, stakeholders care a great deal about the time to market of new products, but the enterprise is presently measuring only development time of products prior to release. The implementation plan might then call for the inclusion of a new measure to address the time to product release. After all, even when a product is developed, there are factors that can hold up its release for market—such as a delay due to a workforce shortage or other delays in manufacturing. As another example, suppose the enterprise is undergoing a transformation to improve the quality of its products. The to-be architecture includes improved processes, infrastructure, and flow of information. In part, the product quality is dependent on a key supplier's performance, but any change to the supplier's processes is outside the scope of the transformation effort. In this case, supplier performance management might be flagged as a risk area, and processes to mitigate can then be developed to minimize impact.

The X-matrix analysis is typically performed in parallel with the detailing of the architecture, given that some additional detail may be necessary to judge the alignment.

We return, now, to the health clinic example from chapter 5. The chosen future architecture is community-centric and focuses on creating value by providing the most convenient services to its select community. This change is reflected in the addition of "convenient services" to both the strategic objectives and stakeholder values in the X-matrix, as highlighted in figure 9.1. Additionally, the misalignments between the strategic objective to manage healthcare costs and metrics, and between and metrics and multiple key processes, were addressed in the future enterprise. The new metrics the architects selected, designed to address these issues, are shown in figure 9.1 (see items highlighted).

Comparison of the future architecture X-matrix with the current architecture X-matrix (shown in chapter 5) reveals the adjustments that have been made in the alignment. These are necessary for successful implementation of the future architecture if the enterprise is to achieve its envisioned future.

Adding Architectural Detail

Detailing the architecture requires thinking more deeply about each of the enterprise elements and their interactions as the implementation is elaborated. It is important for the architecting team to concentrate on adding detail primarily related to "what" versus "how." The latter is left to the design phase where

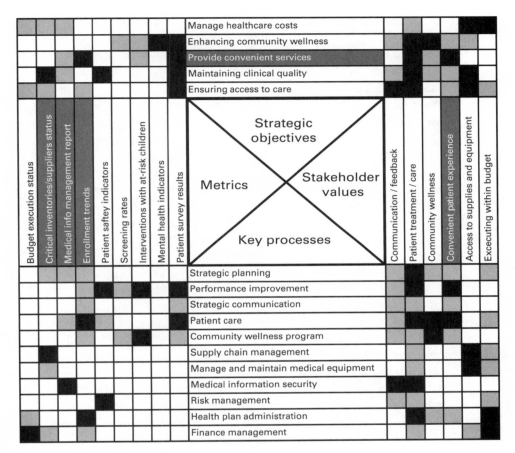

Figure 9.1
X-matrix example for the health clinic future architecture

the team expands to include experts who can best determine the "how." For example, if a new measurement reporting system were to be implemented in support of more extensive collection and reporting of measures, the architecting team would not specify the purchase of a specific available software application in the implementation plan. Rather, they would include an activity to investigate and select such a software application.

The architecting team will likely find it necessary to dig down into some specific implementation-level ideas. This is natural, but it is important to surface back to the concept level, and possibly make informal suggestions on detailed implementation projects and approaches as an adjunct to the plan. The architecture needs to describe all elements at relatively the same level of detail to maintain conceptual integrity in the architectural design.[1] Maintaining level consistency as details are worked out also enables understanding the specific interrelationships of elements. The *element anatomy* is useful for this purpose.

Adding Detail Using the Element Anatomy

Recall the anatomy of an element used to characterize the as-is state of the enterprise (chapter 5). The anatomy of each element was captured for the existing architecture. Given the to-be architecture, we return to the element anatomy, this time to characterize the architecture in more detail. Using the anatomy to elaborate the to-be architecture for each of the eight view elements drives deeper thinking and helps to structure this characterization for understanding differences from the existing architecture.

We suggest using the order of considering elements we discussed in chapter 7 as the view element anatomies are detailed, though in reality there will be a back-and-forth between the view elements in this task.

The strategy element is the place to start. The *structure* is described for the new architecture, noting what is new and what stays consistent with the current architecture. For example, is the business model unchanged, somewhat modified, or perhaps radically changed? Is there any change to the form or type of the enterprise? This might be, for example, going from a limited liability company to a corporation. Is the enterprise going to have a global presence, or will it stay in one national locale?

The strategy element's *behavior, artifacts, measures,* and *periodicity* are detailed in a similar way. Consider a limited liability company moving to a corporate structure, for instance. The architecture will undoubtedly need to drive some new behaviors, like increasing standardization. A new artifact, an annual report, will need to be put in place. Measures that may have been ad hoc will likely need to be more formalized for presentation to a board of directors. The X-matrix analysis may, perhaps, indicate the need for new processes. The management incentives on which bonuses are paid could change to reflect the new strategy. While it is not necessary to fully repeat the as-is enterprise anatomy and mark changes, it is important that any critical retained aspects be noted to ensure clarity. Table 9.1 enumerates some examples of the types of information within each of the anatomical parts of the strategy element, though there are certainly many others.

The process element anatomy is considered next, detailing the new or revised aspects of the process element for the future architecture. The organization anatomy follows. For the organization element, a new architecture might have a functional structure, whereas the current structure is a matrix organization. The number of levels in the organization might be reduced. There could be an accelerated cycle of rotations in assignments.

Table 9.1
Strategy element anatomy examples

Anatomy	Examples for strategy element
Structure	• Business model • Form/type (e.g., NGO, corporation, government agency, etc.) • Global versus "local"
Behavior	• Degree of collaboration • Incentives that drive business performance • Actions in/not in accordance with shared vision
Artifacts	• Strategic plan • Annual report • Core values list
Measures	• Customer satisfaction measures • Percent market share • Financial business measures (e.g., profit, ROI)
Periodicity	• Strategic planning cycles (typically annual) • Strategic plan time horizon increments (e.g., five-year increments) • Pace of enterprise changes

Closely related to the process and organization elements, the knowledge element anatomy for the new architecture is elaborated next. As an example, table 9.2 shows excerpts from the knowledge anatomy of the future architecture selected by a business unit in a very large global corporation.

Next, the products element and the services elements are detailed, followed by the information and infrastructure elements. As the future architecture is elaborated, not every aspect of the anatomy for every element will change. It is always important, though, to be on the lookout for any change that might trigger a need to adjust another part of the anatomy in a given element, or in another element.

One pass-through of completing the element anatomy descriptions provides a good baseline characterization of the future architecture. Cross-checking will be necessary to look for misalignment and gaps. Once the anatomy is detailed, the new architecture will begin to have a rich characterization. Gaps and unresolved areas will be made clear, and strategies can be developed for addressing these during implementation.

Comparing "As-Is" and "To-Be" Anatomy

The two sets of anatomy descriptions, as-is and to-be, are compared to highlight key differences between the as-is enterprise architecture and the selected future architecture.

Table 9.2

Example of the knowledge element anatomy for the future architecture of a global corporation

Anatomy	Knowledge element
Structure	• Communities of practice will be organized as formal groups to share knowledge across business projects.
Behavior	• Leadership will provide incentives for capturing knowledge and best practices to promote a learning organization culture.
Artifacts	• All project "lessons learned" reports will be digitized and placed in the existing knowledge repository.
Measures	• Number of patents per year will now be tracked by the business unit. • Critical skill gaps will be measured on a biannual basis.
Periodicity	• Employee competency/skills assessments will be performed annually. • Corporate hiring policies will be recertified every twenty-four months.

Table 9.3 compares the current-state and future-state organization element anatomy for I-Software Systems, a commercial software product company. This comparison clearly shows what will be different in the future architecture for this particular enterprise.

For example, a revised organizational structure that reflects the reduced levels of management and new, more formal mechanisms for project collaboration require changes. Note that the reduced time for software release decision approval may not only be a function of the new organizational architecture with reduced levels of management approval, but could have implications for the process architecture as well. Similarly, perhaps new infrastructure to replace a paper-based approval process could be part of the solution. In this case, roles and responsibilities may need to be revised. These types of element interdependencies must be taken into account to make sure that all affected elements are updated and aligned.

Considerations for Detailing

Various analytic and descriptive methods may be used to specify the architecture at a next level of detail. For example, Dori's Object-Process Methodology has been used on some of the architecting projects we have been involved in.[2] Maier and Rechtin discuss a collection of representation models for systems architecting, applicable to enterprises as well.[3]

Table 9.3
Organization element anatomy for I-Software Systems

Anatomy	As-is architecture	To-be architecture
Structure	• Functionally organized with formal management hierarchy	• Project-based organization with functional career managers
Behavior	• Collaboration encouraged but happens in ad hoc manner	• Self-directed collaborative clusters within project areas
Artifacts	• High-level department charters exist but are outdated	• Updated charters, with specific project roles and responsibilities
Measures	• Customer satisfaction measured by biannual survey	• Customer satisfaction and employee satisfaction measured annually
Periodicity	• Two-week cycle for software release decision approval	• Three-day cycle for software release decision approval

The architecting team is responsible for establishing the "scaffolding" rather than for working out the detailed implementation plan. Frequently, implementation ideas will come to mind in the process, and these should be captured for future consideration. It is, however, not the architects' role to weave this implementation detail into the plan. Again, the plan developed by the architecting team in this initial phase of transformation specifies "what" the future architecture will be. Architects will not want to elaborate the new product development process without involvement of process owners and subject matter experts. Similarly, architects will not want to research and select a particular PDM (product data management) software application—this requires the expertise of the information technology and engineering leadership. Rather, it is the architecting team's responsibility to determine that the new process will be based on having integrated product and process development, and that the new process will need to be supported by new information technology to implement product data management. This is the level of decisions that the architecting team makes.

Architects are typically involved in, but not solely responsible for, the next phase of the transformation effort, where an expanded team will define the "how." During that activity, enterprises may have specific tools for detailing that they choose to employ. These may include using the Balanced Scorecard, Value Stream Mapping, and various other techniques. This will also be the point where the application of one of the many formal enterprise architecture frameworks may be beneficial.[4]

Implementation Plan

Now, we turn to the critical implementation planning activity. This high-level implementation plan is developed by the architecting team for an important reason, namely, to capture all the thinking and knowledge that have taken place or been acquired over the effort to date. As discussed, it is not atypical for the follow-on detailed design and implementation phases to involve a different set of people—perhaps with some but not all of the architecting team members staying on in this next stage.

Developing a strong implementation plan as the outcome of the architecting process cycle is critical to continuity and future success. All too often a wonderful new enterprise design is created only to languish on the shelf. Or alternately, the architecture is poorly implemented and does not achieve its intended benefits due to lack of effective transition from architects to implementers.

A transformation effort typically spans a significant period of time, and involves and impacts numerous individuals and parts of the enterprise. It often challenges the norms and culture the enterprise has known. The plan must account for dependencies among the activities to be performed during implementation of the new architecture. It specifies the synchronization of the various tasks within and across the various activities. The plan is a tool for keeping a steady course throughout the implementation of the new architecture, in spite of leadership changes that might occur during that period.

An implementation plan is most typically a phased plan for implementing the architecture. Major change rarely happens in a single leap. A typical first step will be to define key projects that will close the gap between the current state and the future desired one. These projects might then be grouped into key "focus areas"—for example, IT systems, policy revisions, process realignment, supplier partnering, and employee development. The designated projects might be further broken down into subprojects to ensure accountability and targeted effort. An implementation plan defines required resources and has realistic timelines and schedules. The plan will include the high-level schedule with all of these projects reflected, along with the interdependencies and critical paths. The next phase, detailed implementation design, will then take these down to a finer level.

Figure 9.2 shows a phased implementation plan. In this architecting case, the first phase was a leadership engagement phase. It included efforts to ensure broad understanding, buy-in, and commitment to the new architecture. The next phase focused on conducting a series of workshops with enterprise experts to detail the specific aspects of the architecture. In this particular case,

Figure 9.2
Example of a phased implementation plan

workshops were held with operations, planning, engineering, and IT groups, followed by a joint workshop to integrate the plans defined by each group for the key projects for implementation. The third phase focused on conducting several pilot projects that came out of the integration workshop. The results of these pilots were used in the fourth phase, architecture improvement. Here the transformation team made any necessary adjustments to the future architecture given outcomes of the pilots. The final phase of this multiyear effort involved the implementation of the projects necessary to fully achieve the future architecture.

Considerations in Effective Implementation Planning

There are a number of considerations for effective planning. First, it is important to recognize that the design and implementation process is iterative, and that there must be feedback explicitly considered and accounted for at frequent intervals in the process. Enterprise change is ongoing. A good implementation plan must provide for adaptations given learning, adjustments to the architecture, and changes to the specific projects. The transformation activities must fit seamlessly with any preexisting efforts that may be ongoing in the larger enterprise. There could be localized improvement activities that are planned or ongoing, and any that are not aligned with the new architecture must be aligned or discontinued.

Another consideration is how to keep the enterprise stable during transition. If there is a lot of change forthcoming, then phasing should allow the enterprise to adjust before taking on more change. In major enterprise transformations, the enterprise needs to have interim stable states to ensure continuous operation in the changing enterprise.

For example, the necessary process and IT infrastructure may need to be established before the enterprise is capable of more innovative new product development or enhanced service levels. Making changes in phases also gives people time to adjust to new ways of doing things by a comfortable pacing of the change process. The enterprise may wish to introduce people to a new

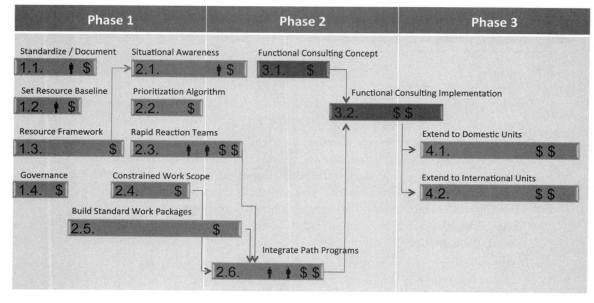

Figure 9.3
Transformation roadmap example

process and gain buy-in prior to undergoing a major reorganization that will result in further process efficiencies.

Figure 9.3 is an example of a high-level transformation roadmap illustrating the big picture of the overall effort. It tells us that this enterprise plans three major phases for the transformation. There are specific activities, where each numbered label (e.g., 1.1) refers to the section in the planning document that discusses the activity. The people icon and dollar sign give us a general sense of whether the activities take more or less effort and funding relative to each other (or possibly correspond to actual levels of labor hours/dollars). Also shown is how the activities flow over time from one to another, as indicated by the directional lines.

Every plan needs to ensure that the required people/organizational capabilities are in place to transform. Experience shows that involving people in designing the change process results in better ideas, greater commitment, and better communication. Good planning efforts take the time to understand who might be resistant to the changes, and build in appropriate mitigation steps. It is important for top leadership to maintain their active sponsorship, enabling the involvement of additional levels of leadership and change agents.

Contents of the Plan

The implementation plan specifies the projects and activities within each of the phases, roles and responsibilities, resource plans, and progress measures. Phases are characterized by the desired outcomes the enterprise hopes to achieve within the specific time period. Within these phases, activities are described along with analysis of their cost and benefit for the enterprise.

Most implementation plans are multiyear plans, so accordingly these plans specify enterprise change in time-based phases. The plan includes the considerations and steps necessary to transform from the current state to the desired future state, including the governance oversight. In multiyear projects the steps in the implementation plan often align with internal strategic plans, as well as driving exogenous factors.

Role of Leadership and Governance

Enterprises are typically quite resistant to change, and maintaining progress over time can be a serious challenge. Transformation works best when persuasive leaders drive the efforts to overcome that resistance. These leaders must have clarity of purpose, good judgment to make sound strategic decisions, effective communication skills, and a talent for motivating others to action. Top leadership needs to communicate the future vision clearly and engage all levels of leadership in the transformation to ensure cohesion and continuity. Additionally, leaders must motivate employees and other stakeholders such as customers and suppliers to participate in the change process. Good leaders can be effective in business improvement, but true enterprise change depends on high-impact leaders with a vision.

Successful architecting relies on the active engagement of leadership throughout the process, and a good implementation plan gives insight into where and when various leaders play a role. Ultimately, enterprise leadership is responsible for making sure that the architecting effort culminates in a plan that is communicated widely and executed according to the selected architecture. Leaders also ensure there are strategic performance measurements in place to gauge success and point to where additional work might be needed. Transition of leadership needs to be designed to ensure continuity in the implementation plan.

Most architecting efforts must also be subject to governance, which is related to leadership but is not the same. Governance is the structure for providing strategic oversight of the effort to achieve results (independent of who the leader might be). It includes ensuring consistent management practices, cohesive policies, guidance, processes, and decision making. While rules are a big part of governance, it is important to note that governance should enable, not create barriers.

Communicating the Plan

An effective plan includes the time and effort necessary for communicating the future enterprise vision, and the action plan to achieve it, to the broader enterprise. The enterprise leadership has a key role in creating this enterprise-wide communication plan. It must be compelling enough to drive the buy-in and participation of the enterprise workforce. It is also likely the plan will need to be communicated, at least in part, to some external stakeholders such as customers, stockholders, board members, or suppliers. It must be solid enough to ensure these external stakeholders believe the enterprise will remain stable during the transition from the current architecture to the new one, and that it will be a better enterprise as a result.

These communication efforts have many facets. First of all the case for transformation must be motivating, with clear strategic goals enumerated. It determines how the "story" needs to be told, including the rationale for change and the benefits that will follow. A vivid description of the desired future should be shared, and the case made for how gaps between the current enterprise and the vision for the future will be remedied. Of course, the case must be made for the level of cooperation and collaboration across the organization that will be part of implementation. The governance plan must give the enterprise workforce the confidence that effective oversight will keep progress going, that resources will be kept in check, and that successful project implementation will be recognized. The plan will outline the frequency and types of progress reporting that will be done both internally and also to the exogenous stakeholders. Communication must have a frequency and style to match the culture of the organization. The use of multiple means of communication has been important in our experience. The diversity of mechanisms may include newsletters, videos, written reports and presentations, town hall meetings, social networking media, and many other formats. The inclusion of at least one mechanism to allow for frequent and ongoing two-way communication is critically important to demonstrate the interest of leadership in having the engagement of the members of the enterprise. Also important is to tell people if and how they will be given an opportunity to be involved in the transformation.

Effective communication gives the enterprise a sense of what to expect as a result of the transformation, and it conveys what members of the enterprise must commit to if the strategic goals are to be met. Once this is accomplished, the architecting cycle is complete. The resulting work is the blueprint for the future, which will guide the enterprise on its journey toward an envisioned future.

Many enterprises have shared with us that this blueprint is the standard against which future decisions are measured. They ask questions such as the following: How does this new idea fit into our future vision, and our plan to achieve it? What else would have to be altered in our implementation plan to add this new item?

This is not to say the plan will never change, because it will. Periodically, in conjunction with the strategic planning cycle or major shifts in the ecosystem, the architecture should be reviewed. Some aspects of the architecture and its associated implementation plan may need to be revised to align with new strategic requirements or shifting stakeholder needs. While it should be a "living" document, it is not anticipated that frequent changes will take place. When changes are indicated, it is important to revisit all the view elements and their interrelationships to ensure alignment and effective and efficient transformation toward your envisioned future.

Developing the Implementation Plan

Exercises to apply to your own enterprise

- Create an X-matrix for your future architecture as illustrated in figure 9.1, realigning strategic objectives, metrics, processes, and stakeholder values as required.
- Develop the future architecture anatomies for each view element (see table 9.2).
- Identify, prioritize, and select key transformation projects.
- Lay out a timed sequence plan for the projects, paying attention to project interfaces and interrelationships.

Questions for consideration

- Are performance measures and processes aligned with the new architecture?
- Who is the executive owner for the transformation plan?
- Who are the key transformation team members and change agents?
- Should the transformation plan be structured into phases to ensure enterprise stability?
- What is the governance model for the transformation implementation?
- What are the mechanisms and frequency of communication?

10   LM Devices Case Study

Our new infrastructure is fundamental to driving our quality processes from manufacturing to design improvements.
—LM Devices executive

LM Devices (LMD) is a medical original device manufacturer (ODM) based in the United States. It is presently a wholly owned subsidiary of SynCo Group, a global employee-owned conglomerate of synthetic materials companies.[1]

LMD produces medical devices, which are then purchased by original equipment manufacturers (OEMs). These OEMs integrate these devices into larger medical systems sold to hospitals and other healthcare organizations. Even though it is a wholly owned subsidiary, LMD largely operates as its own company. It controls its own profit and loss but it does pay a corporate tax levied by the SynCo Group parent company. It does enjoy some of the advantages of being a wholly owned subsidiary—for example, it benefits from the larger corporation's shared services division. LMD medical device products have been in high demand in the last decade, and SynCo Group considers LMD a valuable and strategic business unit of the larger enterprise.

Recently, however, market challenges created both opportunities and some difficulties for LMD, triggering the need for transformation. Several lower-cost competitors emerged in the market, which put some serious price pressure on LMD. The firm began to realize that it needed to focus on specific improvements to support its strategic goals and stem the competition. It set out to aggressively grow its U.S. market share from 25 to 50 percent, and to increase revenue twofold within three to five years. At the same time, LMD wanted to achieve three specific goals: (1) to make considerable gains in product quality; (2) to increase profitability by increasing efficiency and decreasing R&D spending as a percentage of total revenue; and (3) to increase the size and capabilities of the firm to support the market share and revenue growth targets. LMD's existing architecture had allowed the company to reach its current level of success, but would it suffice for what was envisioned for the future? After deep consideration, LMD leadership determined that meeting these goals would require a transformation of the present enterprise.

The Project Begins

LMD initiated a transformation in 2009, beginning with this enterprise architecting activity to select a new architecture to meet the future challenges and take advantage of new opportunities. The primary objective was to effectively address an anticipated significant demand in the market and the opportunities that would result.

The LMD architecting effort was undertaken by a team that included both internal and external members. Once the team had met with the executive leadership to understand the needs and motivation for change, it extensively investigated the current and emerging ecosystem in which the company operates. Following this activity, a stakeholder analysis was performed. These two activities are too lengthy to discuss in full, so we give glimpses here.

Ecosystem

LMD sits within the *global medical device* ecosystem, crossing multiple sectors such as oncology and cardiology. There is a growing global medical device market given greater attention to healthcare and its increased spending on technology. Some of the influences in this growth include aging populations in major markets, and emerging markets and rising income in developing countries. Not surprisingly, the most important external factors that LMD faces in its ecosystem are the regulatory requirements for a medical device manufacturer. These change over time, and also vary based on the nation in which products are marketed and used.

LMD sees 80 to 90 percent of its revenues coming from its top five customers out of a customer base of about one hundred customers. Interestingly, some LMD customers are also competitors on certain product lines. LMD has a proprietary relationship with several OEM customers, making that customer the sole purchaser of a given product. However, these customers often will allow LMD to sell to other customers for noncompeting applications. For example, if LMD supplies a device to a company that does not produce an oncology product with that device, then LMD can sell that to an OEM that will use that part in an oncology product.

Stakeholder Analysis

Once the team had a firm grasp on the enterprise landscape—including both inside LMD and in its larger ecosystem—they began a detailed stakeholder analysis. LMD has five major stakeholder groups:

- *Customers.* OEMs that purchase the devices for integration into a system
- *End users.* Patients and hospitals that use the device (as part of a larger system)
- *Shareholders.* Employees of SynCo Group who have been there over a year
- *Employees.* Employees with under a year of employment at SynCo Group
- *Suppliers.* Raw material suppliers

The architecting team used multiple data collection methods, including stakeholder interviews, review of documentation, and general product market research. The interviews with stakeholders included heads of each functional area in the organization (Product Development, Operations, Quality, Marketing, Sales, and Human Resources), as well as higher-level executives at LMD. Initial interviews were used to evaluate the need to interview additional employees within each functional area. Interviews were also conducted outside the walls of LMD with selected customers and suppliers. The latter were considered very important in that LMD has always prided itself on long-term partnerships.

The architecting team analyzed how its key stakeholders perceived the level of value delivery (low to high) by LMD, as related to its leaderships' perception of the relative importance of these stakeholders. This is shown in figure 10.1.

This stakeholder value comparison brought many insights to the team. The Human Resources (HR) department was seen as having a high level of importance to the enterprise, yet was not treated accordingly. They observed that HR consisted of only a single staff member, clearly inadequate to meet LMD's needs. To grow market share and scale the business, employee recruitment, retention, and development would be critical factors. An HR department with a single employee could not scale the business to the aggressive growth facing LMD.

Operations was struggling to meet customer demand and was dealing with multiple capacity issues. Quality was lagging behind that of competitors and relative to customer needs. The enterprise value delivery to stakeholders had to increase to meet targeted strategic goals. In addition, the emphasis on Product Development and the level of R&D investment were seen as needing to decrease slightly in order to focus on other areas such as Quality, Operations, and Human Resources.

Once the ecosystem investigation and stakeholder analysis were completed to a sufficient scope and level of detail needed to move forward, the team began to investigate the enterprise through the eight view elements. Let's take a quick look at the as-is analysis the team captured for each of these elements.

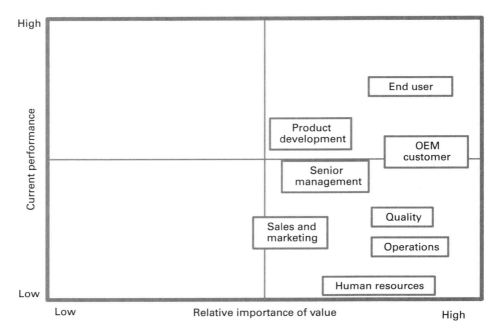

Figure 10.1
LMD stakeholder relative importance versus value delivery

Current Architecture

Strategy

The LMD strategy encompasses the growth, quality, profitability, and scalability objectives described earlier. The process of capturing the as-is architecture revealed some uncertainty about the alignment between strategy and the operations required to meet those objectives. Can existing business operations, for example, even support the desired level of revenue growth? Should LMD consider an acquisition? The future architecture would require some coupling of strategy and the organizational structure required to achieve the objective—something the architecting team noted for its work going forward.

Process

As a maker of scientific instruments, LMD is subject to many industry standards that drive its manufacturing processes, and so these are well defined and documented. Outside of manufacturing, though, each functional area had developed its own processes to meet its specific needs, rarely sharing them across functional groups. Thus, as the process element revealed, little definition or documentation existed. Performance data, while collected, was ineffectively analyzed, which meant the data could not be acted on. This was because, as the process element also revealed, there were few processes to do so and the infrastructure was lacking. As LM Devices grows, this will become an issue. The gap analysis revealed the need for a new architecture that standardized work practices to improve efficiency and consistency, including having processes in place to act on information provided by gathered data. This would need to be coupled closely to changes in the information technology infrastructure.

Organization

LMD, at the time of the project, was employing a total of 120 employees. Approximately 60 percent of these employees were direct labor and 40 percent were indirect labor. The functions included Product Development, Operations, Quality, Marketing, Sales, and Human Resources. Cross-functional collaboration occurred primarily through periodic meetings (e.g., daily stand-up meetings between group leaders). Organizational performance was quantified through managerial tracking of "leading performance indicators," as well as through customer feedback received directly and through an external benchmarking organization. A detailed incentive structure linked each employee's compensation both to organizational performance and personal productivity. The leadership described the culture as compassionate and egalitarian. An artifact of the latter was that all desk-based employees worked in cubicles rather than offices to promote this culture. That said, it was also stated that the culture sometimes lacked accountability and innovative thinking. Furthermore, there was a general aversion to conflict in the enterprise. The analysis showed the need to combat emerging silo effects the team observed in the organization. Leadership indicated a desire to architect a culture to include certain behaviors as the company grew, though specific desirable behaviors were not defined. As part of visioning for the future, leadership would need to identify cultural behaviors it would like to encourage, and then develop specific mechanisms to promote and/or incentivize these.

Knowledge

Knowledge within LMD primarily existed on the part of its employees. Practices were learned on the job and shared as needed with other employees. Management observed some cases of "knowledge hoarding," in which employees were hesitant to fully disclose information that they perceived represented unique value they provided to the organization. Few formal methods of knowledge documentation and transfer were noted. As a result, attrition at the company sometimes resulted in lost knowledge, an issue leadership hoped to mitigate. In addition, a lack of formal documentation of development processes was hindering efficiency, since lessons learned were not necessarily captured and corrected during subsequent development cycles. The architecting team noted that aggressive growth targets would require effective knowledge management to improve efficiency of development, as well as maintenance of knowledge and transfer to new, incoming employees. Moreover, the future-state culture needed to ensure that knowledge flowed freely in the organization to increase speed and agility.

Information

The customer base for LMD products are original equipment manufacturers (OEMs) of larger medical systems, which purchase and integrate LMD devices into a larger medical system used in hospitals and treatment centers. As a result, LMD needs to have current information on the OEMs' systems, including quality problems and planned enhancements. Knowledge of competitor products and pricing is necessary to hold its position in the market. The company must continuously monitor the regulatory requirements and anticipated policy changes across all the nations in which it does business. The current enterprise investigation showed that sales and marketing gathered much of the information that was shared on a weekly basis in meetings. The synthesis and tracking of information were, however, not as structured as leadership would like. LMD was depending on SynCo Group for regulatory-related information, shared on a monthly basis. The team discovered that there had been several times when the monthly cycle of information update was too late for a product decision, creating some rework.

Infrastructure

LMD has production facilities in the northeastern United States and two other countries. U.S. production costs were relatively low because production is highly automated. The non-U.S. locations were observed to have lower automation. LMD was largely utilizing the information technology infrastructure and systems of its parent company. The lack of appropriate IT systems (e.g., Product Lifecycle Management system and Enterprise Resource Planning system) was identified as a significant obstacle to product development and human resources. Since the company's growth objectives hinge on efficiency and productivity improvements, both of which require effective enabling infrastructure, this element revealed that LMD may require some decoupling of its information technology from its parent and tailoring to meet specific needs.

Services

Strong customer service was found to be a key requirement for LMD's ongoing success. These key relationships with top customers had been relatively stable for more than fifteen years; however, management was continually concerned that they could be threatened in the future. As a result, LMD was striving for high standards of on-time delivery and product quality. Customer satisfaction was being tracked both through direct feedback and through an external bench-marking firm. It was noted that 90 percent of customer complaints were quality related, even though quality had already been very high, as necessitated in the medical device sector.

Products

LMD specifically designs and manufactures a line of small medical device (components) for use in larger medical systems. These devices are not useful as stand-alone products, but must be integrated into a larger system by the OEMs. There are four primary product lines produced by LMD. The OEM customers commonly consider the products provided by LMD as commodities. However, the products command noncommodity prices because the competition had not been able to replicate the level of quality and reliability provided by LMD products. LMD was also separating itself through its innovation and product development. This makes it a noncommodity because competitor product replication is very difficult. The product element investigation revealed an inconsistency between the company's strategic goals and the tactics it had established for achieving them. A component of LMD's revenue growth goal included increasing the percentage of revenue from new products substantially, while a component of its profitability goal was to decrease spending on R&D considerably. The leadership would need to evaluate the compatibility of these two objectives prior to agreeing on an envisioned future.

As this part of the architecting effort concluded, the LM Devices team had good insight into the history and trends over a ten-year period. The current state had also been investigated through the ten elements, and the anatomy (structure, behavior, artifacts, measures, and periodicity) of the eight view elements had been examined. Table 10.1 provides an example of the knowledge element anatomy for the LMD as-is enterprise.

The team compiled the as-is enterprise analysis in a report shared with leadership and key stakeholders. This report provided a mechanism for validating the as-is description with relevant stakeholders. It served to increase stakeholder confidence that the architecting team clearly understood the information and perspectives shared with them in the course of the investigation.

Table 10.1
Knowledge element anatomy for LM Devices as-is enterprise

Structure	• Knowledge resident within organizational silos rather than shared • Knowledge resides in peer groups rather than practice communities
Behavior	• "Tribal knowledge" passed down through practice • Some "knowledge hoarding" observed
Artifacts	• Little documentation of accumulated knowledge • Lessons learned reside only in individual engineering notebooks in desk drawers
Measures	• Patent applications per year tracked by the parent company only • Lack of measures to incentivize knowledge sharing
Periodicity	• Knowledge transfer paced by attrition rate • Annual training provided sales force on product enhancements

Vision for Transformation

The architecting team worked with LMD leadership to identify four key imperatives that would be essential to creating the level of enterprise performance the company desired to meet the strategic objectives. These were: (1) create extensive product knowledge through the R&D function and make tacit knowledge more explicit (*knowledge* element); (2) establish independent (from parent) enabling information technology (*infrastructure* element); (3) streamline some processes and formalize others (*process* element); and (4) take the wind out of the silo-effect sails (*organization* element).

Evaluation Criteria

Given the vision for the future enterprise, the architecting team decided on five criteria for the evaluation of alternative architectures:

1. *Flexibility.* LMD needs a flexible workforce, where diverse experience enables people to be assigned to a variety of projects. LMD should also have flexibility in decision making to enable making decisions based on its specific needs, not those of the general corporation.

2. *Scalability.* LMD must be scalable to reach revenue goals set forth by leadership, both in facilities and in the workforce. With factories operating at peak utilization, facilities must be expanded in the not-too-distant future to allow for increased production and product offerings. LMD also has to grow to reach revenue goals from new product offerings. This could be accomplished through various methods, including internal growth through R&D spending or acquisition of an outside company or product line.

3. *Quality.* Quality is very important to any healthcare business because the actions of the company can lead to the injury or death of a patient. Currently, LMD management thinks that product quality needs significant improvement. Another aspect of quality aside from product quality is customer service quality, including on-time delivery. LMD has a history of late deliveries to customers, which can be incredibly bad for customers and patients.

4. *Adaptability.* Adaptability is important because LMD needs to adapt to the changing environment of medical devices, including both market need and FDA regulation. Furthermore, LMD must be able to organizationally adapt as it grows significantly in size. Otherwise, the enterprise will become increasingly inefficient and margins will suffer.

5. *Innovativeness.* LMD must continue with its innovativeness in order to create cutting-edge products that will help it remain competitive in the medical device market. Innovativeness is integral to LMD's business. LMD also needs to be innovative in processes. This will help increase the speed and efficiency of the internal processes, resulting in reduced costs.

Alternative Architectures

About one week after the team completed the concept generation workshop, it commenced the activity to derive alternative architectures. Over the course of two weeks and several half-day sessions, the team developed five alternative architectures that they believed would be able to achieve the strategic goals and future vision of the enterprise.

The five architectures aimed to address the deficiencies of the as-is state of the enterprise, with some architectures addressing various issues concerning dominant views. Given their importance, the team put particular focus on the organization, knowledge, process, and infrastructure elements.

Alternative Architecture 1: Growth through Acquisition

One option for LMD is to grow the firm by acquiring another company in the medical device industry. This purchase could be used to add to their current product line or to increase production capacity to meet customer demand. However, integrating different company cultures could present problems for LMD, and thus a requirement exists to find a company with a similar culture. This architecture could provide a quick path to growth objectives and potentially open new product lines. The following list outlines the view analysis for this architecture:

- **Organization:** Different business cultures could present problems.
- **Process:** Requires standardization of processes.

• **Knowledge:** Will add to the knowledge of the entire enterprise.
• **Infrastructure:** Infrastructure from the acquired company could be used at LMD.

Alternative Architecture 2: Increased Independence from Parent Company

Although LMD does benefit from some autonomy from its parent company, it could seek further independence by gaining more control over capital expenditure decisions such as implementation of new infrastructure suited to LMD-specific needs. One disadvantage of this architecture is that LMD would potentially be required to pay higher fees for some of the shared services it currently receives from SynCo Group. The following list outlines the view analysis for this architecture:

• **Organization:** LMD would still report to SynCo Group, resulting in some limitations and some continuing benefits.
• **Process:** Requires some LMD-specific processes to be created.
• **Knowledge:** LMD will need to create internal knowledge to support its unique processes and infrastructure.
• **Infrastructure:** LMD can acquire its own information technology infrastructure to satisfy its specific needs.

Alternative Architecture 3: Spin Off from Parent Company

A more extreme version of the previous alternative architecture, spinning off from SynCo Group would require LMD to exist as a completely stand-alone firm. This architecture would give LMD the autonomy to run the company completely and potentially also physically separately from SynCo Group. However, new processes would need to be developed for LMD to take on many of the services now provided by the parent organization. The following list outlines the view analysis for this architecture:

• **Organization:** Hire/fire decisions could be made much more quickly.
• **Process:** New processes will be needed after eliminating shared services.
• **Knowledge:** LMD will need to develop internal knowledge.
• **Infrastructure:** LMD can purchase its own IT system suitable for a product development company.

Alternative Architecture 4: Growth through Increased R&D

Although the LMD president believes the current level of spending on R&D is too high, one of the strategic goals it wishes to achieve is to have a higher percentage of revenue derived from new product introductions. This potential architecture explores the possibility of LMD utilizing its capability as an innovator to drive its strategic growth goals. The following list outlines the view analysis for this architecture:

• **Organization:** Will allow R&D to expand as revenue increases.
• **Process:** Enables development of effective product invention and development processes.
• **Knowledge:** May require hiring/growing new types of knowledge.
• **Infrastructure:** Little impact on infrastructure.

Alternative Architecture 5: Cross-Functional Product Teams

To address some of LMD's current issues with departmental silo effects and also to plan for future growth, this alternative architecture aims to reorganize the current team structure so as to have individuals from each core functional group work together on a specific product. This architecture not only aims to eliminate the "silo-ing" of knowledge and information, but should also facilitate communication that ultimately benefits LMD as teams coordinate their efforts more seamlessly. Some new processes will need to be developed to support this effort. The following list outlines the view analysis for this architecture:

• **Organization:** Shift from functionally oriented to project-oriented organization.
• **Process:** Processes will have to be updated to reflect cross-functional teams.
• **Knowledge:** Tacit knowledge will more easily percolate through the company.
• **Infrastructure:** Potential need to adjust facilities to co-locate teams.

Evaluation and Selection

After developing the five alternative architectures the team moved on to evaluation. They employed a weighted decision matrix, developed based on the selected evaluation criteria. Each of the five key enterprise capabilities (flexibility, scalability, quality, adaptability, and innovativeness) was assigned a weight based on the input from a survey conducted with LMD stakeholders. The subcriteria were also assigned weights based on the impact each had on the main criteria. The five possible architectures were then scored on a scale from 1 to 5, with 1 representing no impact or negligible impact in addressing the criteria, and 5 representing the best possible impact in addressing the criteria.

Additional stress tests were run to determine if a different set of weights would yield different results within a feasible range of alternatives (i.e., all five "ilities" had an upper- and lower-bound range of weights the team believed was feasible). Each run, however, generated similar outcomes, with three alternative architectures consistently scoring on top: Increased Independence from Parent Company,

Growth through Increased R&D, and Cross-Functional Product Teams. At this point the team used the output of the evaluation tool as input for deliberation in selecting the future architecture.

Additionally, architecture scorecards were generated for each alternative, using SWOT analysis as a basis. Some informal future-proofing sessions were held to explore how the five alternatives would likely perform given possible changes in LMD's ecosystem during the next decade.

Selected Future Architecture

Following the evaluation, the team combined two architectures (Increased Independence from Parent Company and Cross-Functional Product Teams) into a hybrid solution. This would implement cross-functional product teams, while also implementing a better information technology infrastructure for design and manufacturing. This latter would also provide a degree of independence from the parent company. Based on the strengths of each of these architectures, LMD could eliminate the barriers to communication and increase knowledge flow through the organization by establishing cross-functional teams, along with the enhanced infrastructure for performing their work. Once the hybrid architecture had been selected, the team checked the alignment of strategic goals, stakeholder needs, processes, and metrics using the X-matrix technique (chapter 9). As a result, two gaps were noted and were taken into consideration in the implementation plan. The detail for the selected future architecture was developed through sessions with relevant leadership and technical experts. The team used the element anatomy to prompt discussions and also developed some detailed visual and textual descriptions.

Implementation Plan
A three-phase implementation plan was developed based on the future architecture and on the knowledge gained in the alignment and detailing activity. The first phase involved two key activities. The first was to form cross-functional teams and create enabling processes to support this new organizational model. The second activity was for LMD to negotiate the details of gaining independence through infrastructure changes. This resulted in also needing to change certain affected items such as policies, procedures, and reporting protocols. The team anticipated this phase to take approximately twelve months, with the two activities running in parallel.

The second phase focused on implementing LMD's own information technology infrastructure, enabling it to independently manage design and manufacturing processes instead of relying on the SynCo Group's infrastructure. The team anticipated that this phase would be completed within twelve months. However, a schedule risk was noted in that this is an aggressive goal and infrastructure transitions can be quite complicated and lengthy.

The third phase, planned to take six months, involved extensive employee training for use of the new information technology, data migration, and rollout of the new system. New measures for evaluating the infrastructure usage and positive impacts were included in this activity.

Top-down support is necessary to drive a change initiative of this magnitude. To ensure success, LMD management established a corporate governance structure to approve the plan and monitor its implementation. In addition, a leadership committee was formed to meet monthly to ensure the detailed implementation activities are accomplished and adjusted as necessary. A communication plan was also developed to gain buy-in for the new architecture, and to keep stakeholders (including SynCo Group leadership) informed.

Epilogue

Eighteen months after the architecting effort was completed, LMD finalized its selection of a leading commercial information technology platform. Deployment was planned for all of its manufacturing sites, providing new capability to drive quality processes from manufacture to integrated product design. LMD is implementing the full set of capabilities the new software platform offers, enabling extensive insight into performance and problems.

11   Seven Architecting Imperatives

Every well built house started in the form of a definite purpose plus a definite plan in the nature of a set of blueprints.
—Napoleon Hill

Our hope is that we have now convinced you that architecting is an absolutely essential part of any significant transformation initiative. We believe that effective architecting is a key determinant of the overall success of a transformation endeavor. Architecting leads to better-informed decisions, and increases the likelihood of realizing the potential benefits that can be gained through enterprise transformation.

Seven Architecting Imperatives

As guideposts for transformation, we present seven architecting imperatives (table 11.1) that have evolved from our work with real-world enterprises of varying types, sizes, and missions. While every enterprise may not choose to precisely implement the architecting process as we describe it, we strongly advocate that these imperatives be embraced in whatever path an enterprise chooses to take in designing the blueprint for a transformation.

1.   Make Architecting the Initial Activity in the Transformation Process

Designing a transformation initiative has been said to resemble the task of urban planning. While one part of the living enterprise is undergoing change, it almost certainly impacts some other parts directly or indirectly. The enterprise as a whole must continue to effectively operate while the transformation is ongoing. In this complex and dynamic situation, architecting provides a means to explore possibilities.

Transformation is often initiated in response to urgent and possibly unexpected impacts extending from the changes in its ecosystem. Perhaps a

Table 11.1
Seven architecting imperatives

---

1. Make architecting the initial activity in the transformation process.
2. Develop a comprehensive understanding of the enterprise landscape.
3. Understand what stakeholders value and how that may change in the future.
4. Use multiple perspectives to see the whole enterprise.
5. Create an architecting team suited to the transformation challenges.
6. Engage all levels of leadership in the transformation effort.
7. Architect for the enterprise's changing world.

---

disruptive technology suddenly shifts what stakeholders value, or the ability to trade in a given country opens or closes. A dramatic change in economic conditions or regulatory factors may demand swift action. Given such pressures on the enterprise, there is a natural response to jump immediately into implementing a change. This is almost always a mistake that results in false starts and wasted resources.

We advocate use of an architecting approach to choose the best possible architecture for the future enterprise, all things considered. This can only be achieved by conceiving of alternatives and systematically weighing these against carefully selected, unbiased criteria. Time taken in this early phase of the overall transformation is time well spent.

An architecting approach provides a structured set of process activities to guide the architecting team in an activity that is really more art than science. It expands the space for innovation to occur. It increases the opportunities for effective communication among the stakeholders. The architecting process helps to mitigate risks, and to identify present and future opportunities that can be leveraged. The resulting plan for the future enterprise builds on strengths and closes gaps between current and desired capabilities. Above all, applying an architecting approach at the start of the transformation process significantly increases the probability of selecting the "right" architecture for the future enterprise. The power of architecting lies in generating and evaluating alternatives rather than prematurely jumping to a solution.

2. Develop a Comprehensive Understanding of the Enterprise Landscape

The enterprise landscape is both internal and external to the enterprise, the latter referred to as its ecosystem. It's a common mistake to assume that the landscape is already known, and therefore it is unnecessary to spend time investigating and capturing this knowledge. The landscape is always changing, and the architect's knowledge must be up to date. Further, in our experience, it is rare that any one person has a comprehensive view, and false assumptions can be made.

Time and effort must be devoted to ensuring that the architecting team has a shared understanding of the landscape, both internal and external to the enterprise, before further work is undertaken. Rather than being a general investigation, it must be undertaken to discover those things that are specific to the transformation scope.

As we discuss in chapter 3, the internal landscape includes the ideology, core values, capabilities, and strategic intent. Generally, this internal landscape provides the firm foundation, remaining relatively unchanged in a transformation. We say relatively unchanged in that a transformation may be directly targeted toward a new strategic intent or a desired capability not yet existing in the enterprise. Scope and boundaries determine where the internal landscape ends and the external landscape begins. It is essential to understand these boundaries, because they determine what is under the control of the enterprise and what is largely a constraint.

The enterprise's ecosystem is a living system. It includes all of the relevant constituents (other enterprises) and their interrelationships, which are continuously changing. The ecosystem can be characterized by context factors, including political, regulatory, economic, market, technology, resources, environmental, and demographic factors. Understanding the potential impact of uncertainties in these factors enables better decisions in choosing an architecture fit not only for the present, but also for the future. As we have previously discussed, triggers for transformation often result from a shift of one or more of the context factors in the enterprise's ecosystem. Thriving, and perhaps surviving, means the enterprise must adapt to changes in its ecosystem. It must be able to accommodate shifts in context and stakeholder needs.

3. Understand What Stakeholders Value and How That May Change in the Future

Satisfying stakeholder needs and wants is at the heart of the enterprise's very existence. Yet, time after time, we see that stakeholders cannot always articulate their needs because they themselves may not understand what is possible. They may not think about what they need beyond the current timeframe, or at a deep enough level. This is precisely why we believe taking a value-driven approach is necessary. Getting at what stakeholders really *value*, and how well the enterprise presently delivers this value, is essential. Conversely, the value the enterprise requires from each stakeholder must be determined to understand the complete value exchange. Understanding value gaps provides architects with critical information on where enterprise changes must be made. Anticipating how stakeholder value may shift in the future informs architecture decisions.

As we discuss in chapter 4, the first step in this value-driven approach is to identify the major stakeholders, and to understand the prioritization of the stakeholders in regard to enterprise value delivery. Different stakeholders will often value different things, and these values may or may not be aggregated. Understanding stakeholder value as unique sets of information will serve to invoke the dialogue needed to make difficult decisions in enterprise strategy. Sometimes conflicting needs must be balanced and hard choices made. Stakeholder value has to be understood as it now exists to address value gaps. Architects must consider how value can be preserved and strengthened given the specific transformation effort.

As in the case of the ever-changing ecosystem, stakeholder value tends to shift over time and contexts. What is attractive in a healthy economy might not be in a recession, for example. It is important to keep watch over this. Making uninformed assumptions about present and desired future stakeholder values is risky and may lead to inappropriate decisions in the transformation process.

Architecting teams need to make the best possible effort to understand the relative importance of stakeholders and current enterprise performance in regard to what they value. Gaps can be identified, and anticipated value shifts (both positive and negative) can be discerned. Not all gaps and value shifts can be accommodated, so understanding stakeholder salience can guide the difficult decisions that will need to be made.

4. Use Multiple Perspectives to See the Whole Enterprise

An enterprise is so complex that we can only attempt to comprehend it by understanding it through a parts perspective. Yet, the parts can only really be understood in the context of the whole. Through our research we arrived at ten elements, introduced in chapter 2, as fundamental perspectives necessary to understand the whole enterprise. Ecosystem and stakeholders are the first two elements. The remaining eight are what we term *view elements*. These include strategy, process, organization, knowledge, information, infrastructure, products, and services. Some of these view elements drive other view elements during the architecting process. Some elements may be more important than others in a given transformation initiative.

The ten elements, in combination, are not sufficient to describe an enterprise. These elements must be analyzed collectively rather than individually. The eight view elements serve as lenses for perceiving unique aspects of the whole enterprise. Holistic thinking involves understanding the interfaces and interrelationships of these elements, often the high-leverage points for transformation.

5. Create an Architecting Team Suited to the Transformation Challenges

We cannot overstate how important it is to create the best team possible for the architecting effort. Every transformation is unique. Thoughtful consideration must be given to creating an architecting team that can be effective given the particular needs and challenges of the transformation effort. Architecting involves decisions under uncertainty and with incomplete knowledge. The team needs individuals who can work together under these conditions.

There are several critical aspects to bringing together a good architecting team. Some are about the ways the team functions, while others relate to the characteristics of the individuals who comprise the team. Enterprise architects must be at ease working at all levels of the organization.

First, architecting team members need to represent the diversity of key enterprise stakeholders. And there must be incentives for members to work as a team. Typically, the ideal team's composition strikes a balance between having specialty areas of the enterprise represented and having people who can think beyond their silos about the holistic enterprise.

One of the best ways to build a team with a broad perspective is to have people with experience in more than one of the enterprise's functional areas. At least one team member must be able to see things from the perspective of standing in the various stakeholders' shoes. In creating an enterprise architecting team, then, you must ask which parts of the enterprise and which stakeholders should be represented, and whether the members should come exclusively from within the enterprise, be a group of architecting experts from outside the enterprise, or a combination. While we have seen each of these models used successfully, our experience suggests a team should include at least one member from within the enterprise.

Every enterprise architecting team needs a designated leader, someone who can think strategically and holistically. The person selected to lead an enterprise architecting team needs to understand the strategic intent of the enterprise's senior leadership and be able to relate and translate that intent across the multiple elements of the enterprise. A team leader must be open-minded to the possibilities of what the future might look like, while being grounded in reality.

6. Engage All Levels of Leadership in the Transformation Effort

Architecting emanates from the highest levels of the enterprise and is dictated by strategic considerations. For these reasons, it depends on the active engagement of enterprise leaders responsible for the enterprise strategy. Leaders at all levels play a role, ensuring the conditions and access to information that the architecting team needs to do its investigative and creative work. When leadership engagement is insufficient, time and again, we see architecting teams fail.

Failing to get midlevel management involvement, for example, has meant the demise of many transformations.

Typically, the senior leader or leaders who become passionately involved in enterprise architecting are the ones who have a much-needed "burning platform"— a business term that emphasizes immediate and radical change due to dire circumstances. In fact, without a burning platform, it's the enterprise architect "who may get burned." Accordingly, leadership must provide the architecting team with organizational visibility for its efforts and demonstrate their strong commitment to the broader enterprise.

Every architecting effort requires leadership, and ultimately leadership at the highest level of the enterprise must take ownership and responsibility for the vision of the future enterprise and the plan for realizing this vision. Enterprise leaders, however, rarely have time to undertake an enterprise architecting activity alone. The enterprise needs a team of trusted individuals who understand the strategic imperatives for change, and collectively can represent the stakeholders who will be affected by the transformation. The effectiveness of the architecting team depends on access to, and a collaborative relationship with, the enterprise leadership team.

Enterprise leaders provide a supporting environment for the architecting team. They work with the team to ensure focus on the right objectives and empower the team with the necessary decision-making authority. Leaders ensure that the architecting effort is aligned with strategic objectives and policies, and they direct modifications in these if necessary. They grant allocation of adequate and appropriate resources, including people, money, access to information, and perhaps some analytic and modeling tools. Leadership must provide access to external stakeholders the architecting team will want to engage with in order to understand their thoughts about the enterprise's future direction, constraints, and "must haves." Success depends on having engaged leadership.

7. Architect for the Enterprise's Changing World

A transformation takes time to plan and implement. Meanwhile, the world around the enterprise—its larger social, political, market, and economic context—will be changing. Stakeholder values may shift. Competitors may increase. Policies may change. Markets may open or close. If architects assume a static world, the architectures they design will be sure to meet yesterday's needs.

All too often transformation initiatives are designed without considering that the enterprise exists in a changing world. As the context (economic, political, regulatory, market, technology, demographic, and others) shifts over time, and stakeholder needs change accordingly, there is an impact on the enterprise. Sometimes this impact is positive, creating new opportunities and conditions for growth and financial benefit. At other times, these changes can have negative effects on the enterprise, threatening performance and possibly its future survival. A forward-looking perspective is needed to design an enterprise suitable for an envisioned future. Architectural strategies should be formulated with consideration of possible and likely changes in the world of the enterprise. A long-term view is necessary to generate strategies that will enable the enterprise to both withstand and respond to changes around it. We cannot know the future for certain, but sometimes we can anticipate possible and probable changes in our ecosystem. In this case, we can design the enterprise to be robust and/or adaptable to these changes.

Not all uncertainties can be predicted in advance. As a result, architectures need to be designed to accommodate unanticipated changes in context and stakeholder values, to the extent possible. Future-proofing techniques can help the architecting team generate and select good architectures in the face of a changing world. The failure to do so will result in an enterprise architecture that may be viable in today's world but unsuited to the world of tomorrow. Given the significant investment made in enterprise transformation projects, the resulting architecture needs to withstand the test of time.

Closing Thoughts

Significant progress has been made in broadening enterprise architecting beyond its heritage of information technology and process-intensive practice. Innovations in architecture frameworks, standards, modeling languages, and tools have emerged. These are, however, really only effective if a viable concept is selected before developing a detailed architecture. Unfortunately, this is not always the case. We encourage enterprise leaders to invest in an architecting effort as the essential first phase of enterprise transformation.

Determining the architectural blueprint for the future enterprise is the highest impact decision in a transformation. The ultimate success of the transformation depends on making a sound choice of this to-be architecture. Presently, many enterprises view selection of to-be architecture as a "simple" decision problem. In actuality, it is a decision analysis activity that requires time, appropriate resources, and effort. Effort spent in investigating architectural choices is modest compared with effort spent in recovering from bad architectural decisions.

We live in a time of ever-increasing complexity of both technology and society. The highly interwoven parts of modern sociotechnical systems have inspired an enterprise science. Research on enterprises is increasingly performed by government, industry, and academia, and knowledge is growing. Fundamental theories in management science and systems science from decades ago are experiencing a renewal as architects of modern enterprises reexamine and build on this prior work.

Our approach to architecting the future enterprise has evolved over a decade of applied research. The ARIES framework is the result of the knowledge and experience of enterprise leaders, enterprise researchers, and architecting teams in over 100 diverse real-world projects. Our hope is that this work will guide enterprise leaders in making the important early decisions for architecting their future enterprise in a rapidly changing world.

Appendix A

Architecting Case Study: ISSA, a Business Unit of I-Software Systems

I-Software Systems is a company that sells software, technology products, and monitoring services to businesses of all sizes, governments, service providers, and consumers.[1] The company has been consistently increasing sales over the last ten years and has achieved presence in three continents around the world. Its vision highlights the importance of technology for the world, and recognizes innovation and operational excellence as its core values. To achieve those values, the enterprise invests heavily in R&D.

Architecting Scope

The project highlighted in this case focused on the architecture of a business unit within I-Software Systems, which we refer to in this case as ISSA. ISSA's primary mission is to develop software and provide the architecture that supports the "automation with intelligence" product portfolio, one of the technical services offered by the company. The architecting project was performed in a four-month period, considering a five-year time horizon. This case discusses the architecting project as it unfolded.

Motivation for Change

The major concerns on the part of ISSA leadership relate to the current outsourcing organizations. The architecting team found that managers spend almost 50 percent of their time talking and coordinating with the outsourcing partners over the phone. At the same time, it is common for partners to complain about not having enough information about the product they are hired to produce. The leadership began to believe that a better outsourcing structure might help in improving lead time and cost savings.

The architecting effort was sponsored by a process improvement manager within the enterprise, who was working as an internal consultant for ISSA. The architecting team used a number of methods to gather knowledge prior to engaging with the stakeholders, and examined public reports and information on the external and internal websites. Following this activity, detailed discussions were held with the sponsoring manager to ensure the team had a shared understanding of the desired change.

Enterprise Landscape

Ecosystem (External Landscape)
I-Software Systems has achieved a leadership position in several of the markets where it competes. In the market associated with the services provided by ISSA, the company has a worldwide leadership position with a market share of almost 40 percent. The rest of the market is fragmented across three other competitors. The latest demand trend indicates that the market for monitoring software is growing rapidly, and it reveals an attractive scenario for technological and service suppliers. Despite these numbers, ISSA sales have been growing at a slower pace compared to the rest of the market. This is mainly due to the fact that smaller competitors have been able to react more quickly to market demands, because their product development cycles are shorter and therefore time to market is faster.

Turning to suppliers, the most important suppliers for ISSA products are third-party software developers. In today's scenario, suppliers have relatively strong power due to the fragmented outsourcing strategy of ISSA, as well as the size of the companies that offer these services. Their position is critical to ISSA because they represent around 55 percent of the current workforce used to develop its products. Even though there are several suppliers in the market, the switching costs are high and it takes a long time to reach high levels of productivity (requiring know-how, training, and development of communication channels).

ISSA customers are mainly government agencies, information technology industries, and other businesses, where ISSA products are still identified as the market leader in terms of maturity, reliability, and brand recognition. However, the pace of technology change is increasing and new ways of offering monitoring services could become available in the short term. This may further negatively impact ISSA's market share.

Internal Landscape
I-Software Systems has grown from 100 employees to over 70,000 in 25 years and is recognized as an industry leader in many of the markets it serves. Over its evolution, however, the enterprise capabilities related to timely response to market shifts have weakened, causing overconfidence, cultural and coordination

issues, and a slower response to market needs. Nonetheless, the brand is still very strong and is allowing the enterprise to remain the market leader. Top management is aware of this situation and there is currently high internal pressure on business units to reduce costs and improve the cycle times, in order to recover competitiveness in this regard.

The ISSA business unit consists of around 360 people mainly located in the United States. There is also a small team located in India, with around 20 developers. Additionally, there are five different companies (or partners) where ISSA outsources the programming of its products. The total number of outsourced programmers varies depending on workload, but on average ISSA has 390 outsourced people working on its projects at any point in time. These outsourcing partners are located in China, India, and Eastern Europe, as well as two in the United States.

The ISSA product development cycle is as follows. First, a product requirements document (PRD) is written by the product management team, responsible for regularly gathering customer requirements. The PRD passes through a gate called "executive committee," composed of executives from product and function groups who decide what PRD to approve and begin work on. Five parallel work streams are then initiated simultaneously and resources begin to be allocated. Although there is one overall product manager, he does not carry out the outsourcing decisions. Those decisions are made by each manager of the four teams, as seen in figure A.1. At any one time, multiple PRDs are being worked on by these groups. They look at the availability of resources, deliverables already in process, time estimation, and work with product and the project manager to make sure the schedule is met.

Outsourcing is a key part of the product development process, primarily employed to achieve cost objectives (typically 30 to 40 percent of a project has to be outsourced due to cost). Other reasons to consider outsourcing are the need for specific skills (e.g., a particular programming language) and to meet schedule requirements. There is no consolidation of the outsourcing process; each manager chooses partners based on cost, similarity, or technical skills.

Stakeholder Value

The architecting team's initial task in stakeholder analysis was to identify the major stakeholders of ISSA who could provide insights and information relevant to the internal and outsourcing processes. These stakeholders include

- ISSA director
- Outsourcing partners, including leadership and programmers

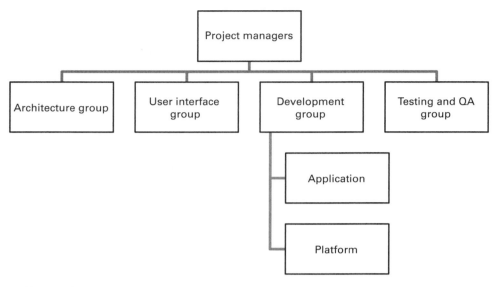

Figure A.1
ISSA project structure

- Architecting project sponsor (independent consultant working with ISSA)
- Employees, including project managers, team leaders, and developers

The architecting team identified the critical stakeholders and conducted interviews with them to understand desired value and current delivered value. For the sake of brevity they are not all included in this section. Results of the stakeholder interviews were synthesized and value delivery graphs showing importance versus enterprise value delivery were developed. The team also created radar plot representations of the same data, since this is a commonly used format in the ISSA enterprise. As an illustrative example of stakeholder value results, the radar plot in figure A.2 shows current performance versus relative importance for seven attributes, for the project manager stakeholder group.

As can be seen, the cost of outsourcing is considered highly important, with high performance. Contrast this with strategic planning, where the current performance is perceived as low compared to its relative importance. Given the composite set of results for all major stakeholders, the architecting team is able to see where the enterprise may be under- or overperforming in response to stakeholder needs. Stakeholders (or stakeholder groups) are not aggregated; rather it is the discussion of the value gaps that contributes the most.

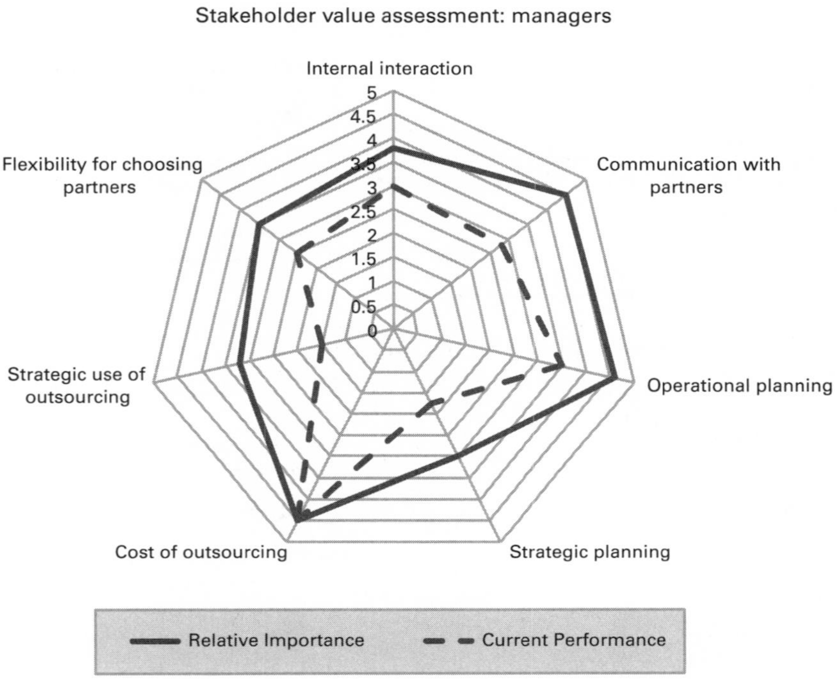

Stakeholder value assessment: managers

Internal interaction

Flexibility for choosing
partners

Communication with
partners

Strategic use of
outsourcing

Operational planning

Cost of outsourcing

Strategic planning

━━━ Relative Importance   ━ ━ Current Performance

Figure A.2
Management stakeholder group value assessment in radar plot format

Current Enterprise

For a better understanding of the as-is enterprise, the architecting team performed a SWOT (Strengths, Weaknesses, Opportunities, and Threats) analysis of
the most relevant elements: strategy, process, organization, and knowledge.
Figure A.3 shows a diagram of the enterprise elements with interrelationship
flows and summarizes some of the key findings from the analysis. For example,
the strategy element analysis showed there was no long-term strategy for outsourcing and tactical decisions were the norm. The process, then, permitted
decisions by different team managers on an independent basis, with weakness
in the coordination and communication. The infrastructure included a decision-
tracking database; however, it was ineffective due to technology-related issues
and lack of process requiring its use. The weak strategy also resulted in fragmented tactical decision-making behavior within the organization.

The architecting team used a *system dynamics model* to better understand the
organization. The team performed some simulations adding more people and

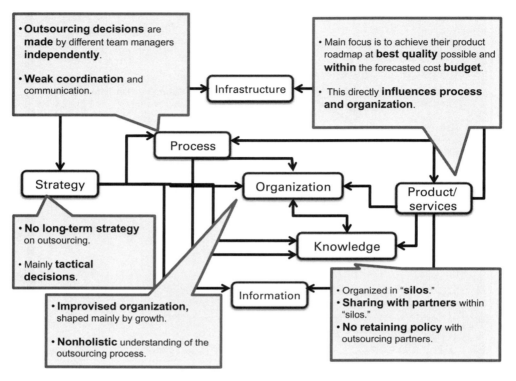

Figure A.3
Selected findings from analysis of as-is enterprise

projects to the current organization. Its main conclusion was that the current architecture was not scalable, because adding many more people and projects will negatively impact the current productivity. Lack of defined procedures and metrics results in negative impact on productivity, therefore increasing delays in projects rather than improving lead times.

Based on the ecosystem and stakeholder analysis, SWOT analysis, system dynamics model, and discussions with sponsors at I-Software Systems, the team concluded that ISSA is executing adequately in its projects. However, it was determined that there were several issues that could be improved through a transformation activity.

The findings were the following. Operations are not in jeopardy at this point; however, there are symptoms of problems that could become real threats for future developments. The main issues the team found were: the outsourcing process is very time consuming, there are communication problems among areas/departments and with outsourcing partners, the current outsourcing structure is about to reach its critical capacity (scalability concerns), there is a weak strategic view of the outsourcing process (tactical decisions), there are no standardized procedures to manage the relationship with partners, there are no metrics to evaluate outsourcers' performance, and there is no clear owner of the outsourcing process as a whole (holistic view). Keeping in mind that the objective of ISSA is to grow at a rate of 18 percent a year, it appeared to be critical to address these issues in order to be successful in the future.

Holistic Vision of the Future Enterprise

The envisioned future guided the team in the next steps and was used as a reference to define the desired attributes of the process of outsourcing within ISSA. To generate the future vision of ISSA, the team worked with the senior management of the unit and considered insights in four major areas: (1) strategic plan, (2) stakeholders' values and priorities, (3) ISSA major drivers, and (4) best practices for outsourcing/offshoring. Taking into account these four major areas, a holistic vision for the to-be enterprise was developed. The vision was designed to align with overall ISSA mission, stated as "To develop highly reliable, affordable and timely solutions for our customers based on operational excellence." The architecting team worked with the senior leadership of ISSA to develop a vivid description of the envisioned future for the business unit, in the form of a news article that would be issued to the press at the end of the five-year transformation activity:

December 31, 2016—Today, software as a service has become the standard for the technology business. This fact and our ability to adapt to the new requirements have made our business unit growth faster than any other competing enterprise. We expect to be the largest service unit in the global market within the next two years. We have been able to keep our operational excellence while expanding our sales more than 20% year after year. Our ability to adapt quickly to new scenarios and strategic alliances with our partners has set this business apart, providing the highest customer satisfaction in the software services market. We have also matured our processes, technologies, and infrastructure to expand our portfolio package from software to cloud computing.

Based on the envisioned future state, the team then defined the particular attributes and desired behaviors that ISSA needed to accomplish to move in that direction. In particular, three dominant view elements were focused on for the outsourcing process: strategy, process, and organization. As a result the team identified thirteen desired attributes for the organization.

Desired Attributes: Strategic Element
• Have an outsourcing structure adaptable enough to support continuous growth in demand.
• Use global outsourcing with a strategic vision that can take advantage of long-term relationships and multiproject negotiations and foster outsourcer understanding of the projects.
• Build long-term relationships with outsourcers, but using short-term contracts that can be optionally renewed after the end of each project. Long-term contracts are more likely to require changes and adaptation, which increases coordination costs.
• Have an outsourcing strategy that allows ISSA to work with talented and experienced contractors within outsourcing firms.
• Work only with providers that ensure competitive labor costs, long-term resource availability, high employee retention, and ideally cultural compatibility with I-Software employees.
• Have a communication plan with major providers that articulates channels and ensures continuous communication on all organizational levels.

Desired Attribute: Process Element
• Work with standardized outsourcing processes that clarify procedures and align practices among different groups within ISSA.
• Have an effective governance model that includes expectations, performance indicators, and clear responsibilities for both the company and the outsourcers.
• Use contracts that are clear in terms of the pricing structure and fees, responsibilities on both sides up front, intellectual properties, rights and restrictions of both outsourcers and company, and liabilities. Exit options should also be included.
• Have an outsourcing manager that owns the process, ensuring that the desired results are defined clearly and reflect the company's true requirements.

Desired Attributes: Organization Element
• Have an outsourcing control system that verifies that results are reported regularly, and that constantly evaluates the outsourcers' performance against an evaluation criterion.
• Have an outsourcing structure able to mitigate risks, allow scalability, and ensure cost savings while protecting quality.
• Have channels of communication on the outsourcing process among different departments.

Comparing the results obtained in the as-is analysis with respect to the desired attributes, the major value gaps of the current architecture were identified for the three dominant views for the outsourcing process: strategy, process, and organization.

Architecture Evaluation Criteria

To define the evaluation method for choosing the preferred architecture, criteria were driven by the two major considerations: they should be able to measure the desired attributes established for the future state using the three dominant elements, and they should address the value gaps identified for the current state.

The evaluation criteria selected by the architecting team were scalability, reliability, manageability, flexibility, cost, and cycle time. The team defined these criteria and broke each down into two quality attribute questions. It then weighted them using a pairwise comparison weighting method. It decided to also include qualitative measurements for "transformability" and "risk" factors.

Concept Generation

The team generated about ten architectural concepts that were evaluated qualitatively. These concepts were sketched during two sessions of roughly three hours each through a structured brainstorming effort.

A qualitative assessment was performed by the team using a simplified SWOT assessment. Four of the ten concepts were found to be infeasible, and two of the remaining concepts were combined into one concept, resulting in five concept architectures to be used as a basis for developing alternative architectures.

Developing Alternative Architectures

Using the knowledge and information gained during concept generation, the team developed four alternative architectures for ISSA. The five architectural concepts were used as a basis for creating the more detailed alternative architectures.

Strong Outsourcing Architecture

One option for ISSA was to strengthen the role of outsourcers in its product development process. This alternative would imply a radical change in the organization because outsourcing partners would take care of the whole process of engineering and testing the projects with the objective of reducing costs and improving communication. Under this architecture, only the product architecture and project management (PM) teams would remain within ISSA. The PM team would be reinforced in order to conduct the additional coordination, evaluation, and control tasks. The outsourcing partners on the other side would be responsible for delivering the products for ISSA.

Backsourcing Architecture

This architecture is exactly the opposite of the previous one. It refers to the action of bringing the existing outsourcing services back "in house." This would imply cutting all outsourcing activities. There would basically be two ways of doing this: (1) acquire one or two of the current outsourcing partners, or (2) gradually hire and create new teams that would take on the task of programming and testing.

Outsourcing Team Architecture

A third alternative is to create a new team/department that will be in charge of the procurement process. This would allow ISSA to concentrate in one group the expertise on contract definition, channels of communication, and bargaining power. For example, with the current process, different areas could be simultaneously conducting outsourcing with the same partner without using their bargaining power. At the same time, this group would be able to have dedicated employees to monitor and manage the performance of outsourcing partners.

This would, however, imply a high implementation cost and would increase the head count of the current organization. Additionally, it would certainly add an extra layer of people (example: engineering manager, outsourcing manager, partner) that could result in longer lead times at the beginning (learning curve and acceptance of new structure by employees). However, if successfully implemented, having a specialized team doing the outsourcing coordination and monitoring would contribute clear and strong governance to the process.

Process Owner Architecture

The current structure of ISSA includes project managers with teams. Each project manager is responsible for the process and schedule governance through the entire product development cycle of each project. However, they are not involved in the outsourcing decisions. The main idea behind this architecture is to empower the project managers in order to have end-to-end responsibility and authority in the process of product development. Having strong process owners allows the organization to be prepared for change and makes people less reluctant to enter new environments. The process focus would allow ISSA to adapt more quickly to the context and therefore increase its chances of survival in a world of rapid change. It would also help align different areas and enable a more holistic view of the process.

In addition, the process manager would define and supervise the outsourcing activities. This architecture should provide better governance of the process and the process manager would be responsible for defining the outsourcing partners, contracts, procedures, and resources allocated in each project. This would allow the centralization of the high-level definitions of the outsourcing process and therefore allow stronger bargaining power with the partners.

Evaluation of Alternative Architectures

Having already determined the evaluation criteria and quality attributes desired for the future architecture, the team set up a weighted evaluation matrix to select the best candidate. For the different quality attributes, each alternative architecture was given a 0-to-5 score. The as-is architecture was included in the matrix to provide a reference for the scoring of the proposed architectures, as shown in figure A.4. In addition, it allowed the team to verify which architectures offer improvements with respect to the current state. As for the criteria, the team used pairwise comparison to define a relative weight for each quality attribute.

Criteria				Candidate architectures				
				As-is	Outsourcing all	Backsourcing	Outsourcing team	Process owner
Scalability	8%	Allows growth while minimizing complexity	50%	3	4	2	5	4
		Long-term relationshop and coordination	50%	2	5	5	5	4
Reliability	15%	Supplier excellence	75%	3	4	5	5	4
		Supplier availability	25%	4	4	5	5	4
Manageability	22%	Use of performance metrics	50%	2	4	5	4	3
		Facilitates communications	50%	2	3	3	4	3
Flexibility	9%	Ability to react to market conditions	100%	3	5	0	4	4
Cost	24%	Labor costs	40%	3	5	4	4	4
		Hidden costs	20%	4	2	0	3	3
		Implentation costs	40%	5	0	0	1	4
Cycle time	22%	Improves delivery compliance	65%	3	3	5	4	4
		Facilities lead-time reduction	35%	4	3	3	4	5
				3.1	3.41	2.86	3.89	3.81
Ranking				4	3	5	1	2
Risk and transformability				✔	✘	✘	★	✔

Figure A.4
Weighted decision matrix

Two distinct "winning" architectures had very close scores: Outsourcing Team with a score of 3.89 and some risk, and Process Owner with a score of 3.81 and less risk. Based on the purely quantitative results obtained using the evaluation metrics, the preferred architecture would be the Outsourcing Team option. However, two additional factors had to be considered in this decision:

1. Risk: The ISSA management is risk averse and therefore prefers introducing gradual changes into the organization.
2. Transformability: This encompasses impact on current structure, cultural values, and resistance to change.

Given these factors, and considering that the quantitative difference between the two options was minimal, the team's recommendation was to proceed with the runner-up alternative: the Process Owner option.

Deciding on the Future Architecture

The primary goal of the selected architecture is to empower project managers to have end-to-end responsibility and authority over the process of product development. Adapting ISSA to this structure would allow gradual changes in the organization, and if successful this could facilitate the future adoption of a second architecture for deeper change. Therefore, the strategy selected was to use the Process Owner Architecture as a bridge for achieving longer-term goals with subsequent implementation of the Outsourcing Team Architecture. The benefit of this approach would be achieving growth goals defined for ISSA (between 15 and 20 percent), and building support for a more centralized outsourcing group. Finally, if an outsourcing team was to be implemented, the architecting team's recommendation was to aim to standardize the practices and procedures with those of other procurement teams within the whole company, because I-Software Systems lacked a unified procurement system.

Future Proofing
To test the suitability of the selected architecture for the future, four potential scenarios that ISSA could face in the years ahead were elaborated: (1) increasing labor costs in India and China, (2) downturn in the U.S. economy, (3) unexpected growth in demand for I-Software products, and (4) a major outsourcing partner becomes a competitor. The team did not propose a particular order for these four scenarios, but aimed to see what common guidelines would help ISSA be successful in all four cases.

The main conclusion obtained from this analysis was that having an organization responsible for the outsourcing process not only helps to achieve operational excellence but also gives the organization a key resource with which to succeed. The process owner and/or outsourcing team would be quicker to react and adapt to changes in both stakeholder needs and environment. For example, developing and monitoring metrics could help them anticipate changes and therefore be proactive. As noted, this analysis stresses the need for an approach of implementing a Process Owner Architecture as a bridge to later evolving to the Outsourcing Team Architecture.

Following the testing of the architecture in the context of possible futures, the architecting team validated the architecture. This involved review with leadership and other key stakeholders to assess if the selected architecture strategy met their needs, recognizing that these may shift somewhat over the course of the architecting effort given dynamic changes in the world, and recognizing that new understanding may have resulted through participation in the architecting effort.

Implementation Plan

Given the decision, the team proceeded to detail the Process Owner Architecture. This included detailing the elements using the anatomy (structure, behavior, artifacts, metrics, and periodicity). The results from validation led to minor enhancements to the architecture that were also elaborated in further detail.

For the implementation process the team aimed to address the major questions that a manager might have: What are the steps? How long will it take? What are the benefits? Three major phases for the transformation were outlined (table A.1): preparation taking six months, implementation of the interim

Table A.1
Three-phase implementation plan

Phase	Activities
Preparation	• Leadership engagement • Communication with ISSA • Architecting workshops • Developing outsourcing metrics • Pilot project activities
Implement Process Owner Architecture	• Selection of process owners • Training of process owners • Realignment of organization structure • Rollout and communication with leadership and workforce • Monitoring and adjustments
Implement Outsourcing Team Architecture	• Creating outsourcing team • Analyzing merger of outsourcing group with other I-Software Systems business units • Communication of results • Monitoring and adjustments

architecture taking eighteen months, and the subsequent Outsourcing Team Architecture implementation over three years.

Key aspects of the implementation process include involvement of people (from directors to employees), continuous monitoring, as well as feedback and communication of results to praise successes and correct mistakes.

Epilogue

I-Software Systems leadership approved the ISSA architecting strategy with minor revisions. ISSA implemented the Process Owner Architecture following refinement of the architecture based on leadership directions and performance of the preparation activities. The Outsourcing Team Architecture has been successfully implemented, with some adaptation, given technology-driven priorities and opportunities.

Note

1. I-Software Systems and ISSA are fictitious names for an actual enterprise that was the subject of this study.

Appendix B

Architecting Case Study: Allan Design Group

Allan Design Group (ADG) is an architectural firm in a major city in the United States. The firm has been in existence for over one hundred years and has gone through several evolutions in its history. It currently operates in the healthcare and higher education industries, designing large-scale buildings such as medical office buildings, specialty clinics, classroom buildings, and student housing. Services that ADG provides include architecture, planning, renovation, and programming to prioritize the requirements of multiple stakeholders in providing comprehensive solutions.

Motivation for Change

ADG decided to undertake an enterprise architecting project to help the firm gain an understanding of its strategic issues and objectives, now and a decade into the future. The firm wished to develop a future vision for ADG that will deliver value to stakeholders in response to business/organizational needs and drivers. This vision is focused on evolving the enterprise as it faces an increase in competition. The firm wishes to continue to grow and sees a number of different types of opportunities to do so. Accordingly, leadership is seriously considering expanding the current business model.

Ecosystem

The ADG enterprise architecting team investigated the ecosystem by means of a technique commonly used in the firm. This technique is a form of *force field analysis* used to understand key drivers both for and against change.[1] Their analysis focused on architecture and engineering (A/E) firms and construction industries (including the important issue of environmental sustainability), as they relate to ADG.

Table B.1

Force field analysis for architecture and engineering (A/E) firms

Drivers for change	Drivers against change
Engineering: 3%–5% growth in education and healthcare within one year	Economic uncertainty
Healthcare a promising industry, given an aging population	Ability of clients to get project funding
Increase in public-private partnerships	Pressure to reduce fees given increasing competition
Growing need for engineers in architecture projects	Focus on revenue and growth may diminish quality
Architecture and construction show a 10% annual growth in nonresidential buildings	Midsize firms squeezed out due to high overhead fees

Table B.1 shows the force field findings for A/E firms. Growth in educational and healthcare projects appears promising in both the short and long term, particularly given an aging population that will demand more healthcare facilities in the future. However, given the economic uncertainty, clients are having difficulty getting financing for their projects, and A/E firms are under pressure to reduce fees. Therefore, while pursuing educational and healthcare building projects is economically sound in the long term, there is certainly a need to consider how ADG can further position itself in this competitive industry.

A force field analysis was also done for the construction industry. This provided some useful insights, since the firm is affected by the forces that affect the building construction industry. Population growth, particularly in urban areas, is undoubtedly going to drive growth in institutional building construction, requiring more A/E firms. This growth will be particularly large in emerging markets, although ADG indicated that it did not wish to pursue international opportunities at this time, given the complexities associated with delivering these projects. In addition, there is a focus on constructing modular buildings (i.e., assembling building segments first on the ground and then lifting them into place with a crane). This change could be a threat to ADG's "customizable" approach to designing buildings according to client needs.

Overall, this analysis suggests that it is economically sound in the long term to continue to focus on the higher education and healthcare markets, but that there are some challenging areas as well, notably the increase in modular design as well as the challenges in getting building owners to take a lifecycle view of their buildings.

Table B.2

ADG's major stakeholders

Class of stakeholders	Stakeholders
Primary beneficiaries	Client organization officers
	Client facility managers and operators
Beneficial stakeholders	Client project managers
	ADG group officers
	ADG principals
	ADG employees
	Consultants/partners
Charitable stakeholders	End users
High-leverage stakeholders	Investors/donors

Stakeholder Analysis

The architecting team identified the primary stakeholder groups as summarized in table B.2.

The client typically maintains a small project management office that reports to senior executives to coordinate the proposed project. Because ADG does not maintain engineers and landscape architects on staff, it must hire consultants with specialties in civil/geotechnical engineering (for site work), structural engineering, MEP/HVAC engineering (mechanical, electrical, and plumbing / heating, ventilation, and air-conditioning), fire safety engineering, and landscape architecture. ADG often hires technical experts, such as code consultants, to ensure that the building design meets applicable building codes.

The architecting team examined the value exchange between stakeholder groups and the enterprise, including both value expected from the enterprise and value contributed to the enterprise. This analysis (as described in chapter 4) provided a method to examine the performance of ADG against what is important to its stakeholders. The team enhanced its analysis by categorizing the needs in six areas: money, knowledge, services, resources, information, and relationships.

Looking at the whole of this analysis, the team concluded the future architecture must provide for gaining more insight into the strategic direction of clients so that it can better tailor its services. ADG clearly perceives that it could improve on both creating and maintaining longer-term relationships with clients (although this issue is not universal across all clients).

Current Enterprise

The current ADG strategy is to broaden its existing service portfolio and add new services to its portfolio of offerings. The architecting team talked with leadership on their strategic imperatives for change. The CEO expressed a desire to expand upstream (e.g., strategy and planning) and downstream (e.g., commissioning and maintenance) from the enterprise's current offerings, as opposed to expanding laterally into providing engineering and construction services.

Looking forward five years, ADG leadership expressed a second imperative to be in a position in which they can be more selective on clients to work with, such that they can provide intellectually stimulating tasks for their employees (and improve retention of employees in a highly competitive climate).

As it looked at the current enterprise, the architecting team came up with the conceptual framework shown in figure B.1, to understand the as-is architecture of ADG as well as to use later in developing the alternative architectures.

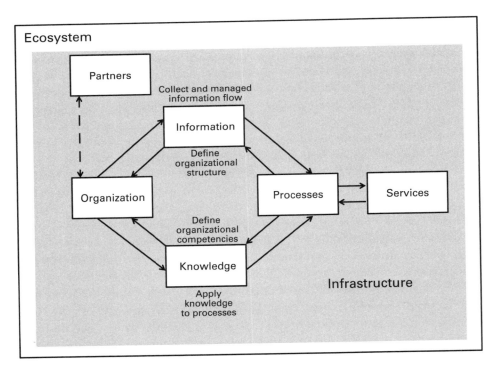

Figure B.1
Framework for looking at the current and alternative architectures

ADG is ultimately responsible for delivering services to its clients. Reading the figure from left to right (i.e., starting at organization) makes it possible to grasp how ADG's organization delivers these services by channeling information, from clients and subconsultants, and knowledge, from its employees, into processes that deliver its services. Since the organization, including its partners (i.e., subconsultants), largely structures how the services are delivered, it is shown at the "top" of this hierarchy leading to services. Therefore, by looking at the figure from left to right, it is possible to better understand why the as-is architecture is configured as such. Since one strategy ADG uses is to create new services to give it a competitive advantage, services is the starting point in the A/E process.

Holistic Vision of the Future

The architecting team organized a session with ADG leadership to develop a vision of the future, looking out five years. A vivid description was created, as shown below, and vignettes were developed to elaborate that vision (as we discussed in chapter 6).

After 110 years, Allan Design Group has transformed from an architectural services firm and into a full service design consulting firm. The firm's recent work displays its wide range of knowledge across the entire building lifecycle, from strategic planning to building design to facilities optimization services. The firm differentiates itself by deploying a diverse team and the use of a customized approach to tackle the specificities of the project at hand. ADG solutions have increased profitability standing and performance for their clients, most notably in the healthcare, higher education, and biotechnology sectors. (Architectural Press, June 2018)

Concepts and Alternative Architectures

With the vision established, the architecting team held a session to come up with concepts, extract the desired attributes, and group these using the view elements. Using this analysis as input, four alternative architectures were developed for further consideration: (1) planning/facilities redesign consultants, (2) flexibility consultants, (3) human factors design consultants, and (4) operations and organization design consultants. Highlights of these architectures are explained below.

Planning/Facilities Redesign Consultants

The planning/facilities redesign architecture alternative essentially involves conceptual design services for facility renovation and master planning—in order to optimize space and land utilization given best-practice design and budgetary considerations—throughout the project lifecycle. In general, the healthcare and educational market sectors would be targeted, which are the priority markets with respect to ADG strategic plans.

Flexibility Consultants

This architecture falls within the realm of more traditional markets such as industrial companies and laboratories. The services offered would include modeling and scenario planning while engaging with the client to determine what could be built for functional use at the present that could scale to accommodate added structures. An example is a parking garage design that would involve a phased approach with budgetary considerations in which two stories would be built today with options for additional stories in the future. This would facilitate long-term client engagement, because ADG could continue to engage with the client over time to determine when it could be useful to exercise the flexibility that was designed into the building.

Human Factors Design Consultants

The human factors design consultants alternative essentially involves designing for human use through the implementation of user-centered design practices. This candidate architecture would have considerable user involvement in various phases of the design lifecycle process for the incorporation of user preferences and validation of the concepts developed. It would include human factors evaluation methodologies to ensure an optimal user experience with the final deliverable. This candidate architecture would provide Allan Design Group with new market opportunities.

Operations and Organization Design Consultants

The operations and organization design alternative would incorporate enterprise architecting and systems thinking in ADG design service options. This would involve the use of architecture or physical space to strategically engender paradigm shifts or changes in an enterprise. It would include the incorporation of financial considerations. This would provide ADG with opportunities in traditional and new markets.

Evaluation and Selection of Alternative Architectures

The four candidate architectures were evaluated using an unweighted Pugh matrix, with criteria mapped to stakeholders (figure B.2). An overall implementability score was given, using a scale of easy, moderate, and difficult. Given

Stakeholders	Criteria	Alternative architectures				
		Facility design consultants	Flexibility consultants	Human factors design consultants	Operations organization design consultants	Research and development
Employees, officers	Flexibility with human resources	0	0	0	0	0
Clients, officers	Flexibility with project customization	0	+1	+1	+1	0
Employees, officers	Compatibility with current competencies	+1	+1	0	0	−1
Officers	Adaptability of new competencies	0	+1	+1	+1	+1
Clients, officers	Affordability for firm and clients	+1	+1	−1	−1	0
Clients, officers	Replicability and reliability of services	+1	+1	+1	−1	0
Clients, officers	Long-term client relationships	0	+1	+1	+1	−1
Employees, principals	Innovatability	0	−1	+1	+1	+1
Employees	Draw for current and future culture	0	0	+1	+1	+1
	Total +1	3	6	6	5	3
	Total −1	0	1	1	2	2
	Total 0	6	2	2	2	4
	Total Score	3	5	5	3	1
	Overall implementability score	Easy	Easy/ moderate	Moderate/ difficult	Moderate	Moderate

Figure B.2
Unweighted decision matrix for four architectures and additional R&D alternative

both the criteria scores and the implementability, the team concluded that the results indicated that the flexibility consultancy was the preferred architecture. As often happens, when the team discussed the results with ADG leadership, it became clear that the flexibility consultancy service would require them to target a market in which they currently have no strong experience (real estate development) and that is already saturated. Although attractive, it seemed too risky to take on at this time. As a result, a final decision was made to select the operations and organization design consultancy architecture. Discussions also spurred the idea of developing an R&D group that could take existing product ideas that ADG develops during a project, and develop and patent them for licensing. As a result, the selected future architecture was enhanced to include this aspect.

Details and Validation of "To-Be" Architecture

After selecting the future architecture, the architecting team detailed it using the view elements. In particular, it focused on the service view (because that was the focal point of this study), as well as on the knowledge and process views (since changes in these elements are important for establishing the new services).

While the operations and organization consultancy will offer customizable services to external clients similar to ADG's existing services, the R&D service is an internal service that will require using standardized processes to ensure that important steps are not missed in the patenting process. Both of these

Table B.3
Selected architecture with anatomy (excerpts) detailed for three elements

	Services	Processes	Knowledge
Structure	Custom services unbundled from architecture practice	Cross-departmental generalized approach, with high-level standardization	Knowledge-sharing system—internal (some external consultants as needed)
Behavior	Collaboration with clients to tailor services	Working in teams with clients	Open internal knowledge sharing, and designed incentives
Artifacts	Contracts and client reports	Client memos, reports, and literature	Documented best practices and lessons learned
Measures	Client satisfaction, profitability, and number of projects	Project budget and schedule metrics, as well as revenue projections	Competency measures and number of certifications
Periodicity	Service delivery cycle time	Business development review frequency	Website update cycles

new services will need to be supplemented by enhanced knowledge- and information-sharing platforms, to ensure that knowledge generated in these new practices is shared across the company. In particular, in the case of the R&D service, sharing new product ideas from the existing architecture practice to the new R&D group will be critical to the viability of this business. For new services, ADG plans to pursue a combination of new hiring and training existing staff. As a result, most importantly, human resource processes will need to be enhanced to identify knowledge gaps and determine how to appropriately fill them.

The project team also detailed key interactions by describing the service view element, before using it to drive the contents of the other views. There are a few notable interconnections within the architecture worth discussing. To offer an enterprise design consulting service, ADG must continue to use flexible processes that are customizable for each of its clients, which is consistent with its existing service offerings. In addition, although ADG will need to develop new processes in order to offer these services (particularly in regard to any training that it will need to provide its clients), many of the processes will be very similar to the ones it uses for its existing design services. By contrast, for R&D, ADG must develop standardized processes to ensure that important steps in the development and patenting process do not fall through the cracks, which might conflict with its existing "creative" culture. Therefore, careful thought will need to be given to ensure these new processes do not stifle the creativity of the existing design process.

Another notable interconnection occurs between the knowledge and organization views. Because ADG wishes to leverage its existing domain knowledge and architectural services in the healthcare (and higher education) fields for its enterprise consulting services, it is leaning toward slowly building up its competencies through both in-house training and hires. Alternatively, it could also potentially grow this service by hiring a new principal, who already has a portfolio of contacts, but integrating someone with their own niche into the existing organization would likely be much more difficult unless the individual was an excellent fit. In addition, according to ADG leadership, it takes over a year for a new principal to be bringing in revenue for the company. Because ADG values consistency in service and with its existing culture and brand, it is likely to pursue a more organic growth strategy to build up its competencies. This strategy will also allow it to continue to use teams that bring together different competencies and skills from across the organization.

Implementation Plan

The architecting team used the detailing information to inform the development of the implementation plan. The plan includes three major thrusts over three to five years, as ADG develops the required capabilities to meet the needs of its client base. These are: enhance the ADG value proposition through the introduction of new services; increase the overall profitability of the company; and create a more dynamic and rewarding workplace for employees. To achieve these objectives a set of overlapping activities are mapped out, using three concurrent project areas, including (1) redefinition of the human resource area, (2) implementation of the R&D process, and (3) full implementation of the organization/process consultancy.

Epilogue

The enterprise architecting team hired by ADG successfully completed the objectives of the project. Leadership gained a deeper understanding of the strategic architectural issues and objectives of their firm. From this understanding and analysis of the current architecture, a vision for the future of ADG was generated in a collaborative workshop. Several alternatives were developed and evaluated. This prompted significant discussion with the ADG leaders, and a future architecture was decided on. The team developed a high-level implementation plan as a guide for further planning of a transformation to achieve the vision and strategic imperatives over the next decade.

Note

1. Force field analysis used by ADG is based on the work of Karl Lewin in the 1940s. The forces in the ecosystem are examined in regard to whether they are positive forces, moving the enterprise toward its goals, or negative forces that work against achieving its goals.

2. Allan Design Group is a fictitious name for an actual enterprise that was the subject of this study.

Notes

Chapter 1

1. *Enterprise* is the term we use in our work. Others may instead use *organization, firm, establishment, company,* or other terms. An enterprise may be a company, an establishment, a firm, a not-for-profit, a nongovernmental organization, a government agency, a university, a social enterprise, or any of the many other types of enterprise entities.

2. "A system is an organized, purposeful structure that consists of interrelated and interdependent elements (components, entities, factors, members, parts etc.). These elements continually influence one another (directly or indirectly) to maintain their activity and the existence of the system, in order to achieve the goal of the system" (BusinessDictionary.com, 2012).

3. D. J. Nightingale, "Principles of Enterprise Systems," paper presented at the Second International Symposium on Engineering Systems, MIT, Cambridge, MA, June 15–17, 2009.

4. V. Purchase, G. Parry, R. Valerdi, D. J. Nightingale, and J. Mills, "Enterprise Transformation: Why Are We Interested, What Is It, and What Are the Challenges?," *Journal of Enterprise Transformation* 1, no. 1 (2011), 14–33.

5. S. Woo, "Under Fire, Netflix Rewinds DVD Plan," *Wall Street Journal*, October 11, 2011, http://online.wsj.com/news/articles/SB10001424052970203499704576622674082410578.

6. For example, on the interrelationship between strategic goals and objectives and organizational processes as additional critical success factors in ERP implementations, see H. Akkermans and K. van Helden, "Vicious and Virtuous Cycles in ERP Implementation: A Case Study of Interrelations between Critical Success Factors," *European Journal of Information Systems* 11 (2002): 35–46.

7. D. J. Nightingale and D. H. Rhodes, "Enterprise Systems Architecting: Emerging Art and Science within Engineering Systems," MIT Engineering Systems Symposium, 2004, http://esd.mit.edu/resources/symposium2004.html.

8. One root cause of this is the failure to sufficiently educate enterprise leaders appropriately, as discussed in: D. H. Rhodes and D. J. Nightingale, "Educating Services Science Leaders to Think Holistically About Enterprises," in *Services Science, Management and Engineering* (Bill Hefley and Wendy Murphy, eds.), New York: Springer, 2008.

Chapter 2

1. On the history of the term *enterprise strategy*, see M. Meznar, J. Chrisman, and A. Carroll, "Social Responsibility and Strategic Management: Toward an Enterprise Strategy Classification," *Academy of Management Proceedings* 1 (1990): 332–336.

2. R. Edward Freeman, *Strategic Management: A Stakeholder Approach* (Boston: Pitman, 1984).

3. J. Schekkerman, *How to Survive in the Jungle of Enterprise Architecture* (Bloomington, IA: Trafford Publishing, 1994).

4. William Rouse has written many books and articles on enterprise transformation. These include W. B. Rouse, "Enterprises as Systems: Essential Challenges and Approaches to Transformation," *Systems Engineering* 8 (2005): 138–150; W. B. Rouse, "A Theory of Enterprise Transformation," *Systems Engineering* 8 (2005): 279–295; and W. B. Rouse, ed., *Enterprise Transformation: Understanding and Enabling Fundamental Change* (Hoboken, NJ: Wiley, 2006).

5. Eberhardt Rechtin, *Systems Architecting: Creating and Building Complex Systems* (Englewood Cliffs, NJ: Prentice Hall, 1991).

6. "Eberhardt Rechtin: An Interview Conducted by Frederik Nebeker," February 23, 1995, IEEE History Center, http://www.ieeeghn.org/wiki/index.php/Oral-History:Eberhardt _Rechtin.

Chapter 3

1. Ricardo Valerdi, Deborah Nightingale, and Craig Blackburn, "Enterprises as Systems: Context, Boundaries, and Practical Implications," *Information Knowledge Systems Management* 7, no. 4 (2008): 377–399.

2. Adapted from Adam M. Ross, "Managing Unarticulated Value: Changeability in Multi-Attribute Tradespace Exploration," doctoral dissertation, MIT, 2006.

3. T. Fischer, H. Gebauer, and E. Fleisch, *Service Business Development: Strategies for Value Creation in Manufacturing Firms* (Cambridge: Cambridge University Press, 2012), especially 16–17.

4. N. Islam and S. Ozcan, "Disruptive Product Innovation Strategy: The Case of the Portable Digital Music Player," in Ndubuisi Ekekwe, ed., *Disruptive Technologies, Innovation, and Global Redesign: Emerging Implications*, chap. 3 (Hershey, PA: IGI Global, 2012).

5. Starbucks Corporation, *Starbucks Global Responsibility Report: Year in Review: Fiscal 2010*, http://globalassets.starbucks.com/assets/2660085bf62e4246a91a8024f500cb37.pdf, and Starbucks Corporation, *Starbucks Global Responsibility Report: Year in Review: Fiscal 2011*, http://www.starbucks.com/assets/19c68ea6c48a473d865c7327c08d817f.pdf.

6. Deere & Company, "Core Values," 2014, http://www.deere.com.

7. J. Diaz, "Small Touches Make Things Clear," *Boston Globe*, October 15, 2011, B.5.

8. The definitions of capabilities (ilities) we use are indebted to the work of MIT research scientist Adam Ross. The importance of a precise definition of ilities is discussed in A. M. Ross, D. H. Rhodes, and D. E. Hastings, "Defining Changeability: Reconciling Flexibility, Adaptability, Scalability, Modifiability, and Robustness for Maintaining Lifecycle Value," *Systems Engineering* 11, no. 3 (2008): 246–262.

9. Starbucks Coffee Company, "Starbucks Reinvents the Store Experience to Speak to the Heart and Soul of Local Communities," June 25, 2009, http://news.starbucks.com/news/starbucks-reinvents-the-store-experience-to-speak-to-the-heart-and-soul-of-.

Chapter 4

1. Earll Murman et al., *Lean Enterprise Value: Insights from MIT's Lean Aerospace Initiative* (New York: Palgrave, 2002).

2. Jody Hoffer Gittell, *The Southwest Airlines Way* (New York: McGraw-Hill, 2003).

3. Theodore Piepenbrock, "Toward a Theory of Evolution of Business Ecosystems: Enterprise Architectures, Competitive Dynamic, Firm Performance, and Industrial Co-Evolution," doctoral dissertation, MIT, 2009.

4. Ronald K. Mitchell, Bradley R. Agle, and Donna J. Wood, "Toward a Theory of Stakeholder Identification and Salience: Defining the Principle of Who and What Really Counts," *Academy of Management Review* 22, no. 4 (1997): 853–886.

5. Ignacio Grossi, "Stakeholder Analysis in the Context of Lean Enterprises," master's thesis, MIT, 2003.

6. Douglas Matty, "Enterprise Management System for the U.S. Army," doctoral dissertation, MIT, 2010.

Chapter 5

1. A recent use of enterprise elements in examining enterprises is discussed in Andrea Ippolito, "Architecting a Future Tele-Health Care System to Treat PTSD in the US Military," MIT SDM Systems Thinking Webinar Series, January 13, 2014, http://sdm.mit.edu/news/eventsarchive.html.

2. The importance of seeing an enterprise as a whole system is discussed in Jordan Peck, "Optimizing Performance in the Modern Health Care Delivery System," doctoral dissertation, MIT, 2012.

3. The relationships among enterprise views in hospital performance are discussed in Jorge Oliveira, "High Performing Hospital Enterprise Architectures," doctoral dissertation, MIT, 2011.

4. Note that the Starbucks example is drawn from publicly available literature, news releases, and the corporation's website and may not represent the current and actual business features, nor does it necessarily represent the actual views of the corporation. It is simply for illustrative purposes.

5. McCafe is a coffee-house-style chain, owned by McDonald's, which was started in 1993 in Australia and first opened in the United States in 2001.

6. More information on the X-matrix can be found in Deborah J. Nightingale and Jayakanth Srinivasan, *Beyond the Lean Revolution: Achieving Successful and Sustainable Enterprise Transformation* (New York: AMACON, 2011), 114–118.

Chapter 6

1. WP Guidance Corporation is a fictitious name for an actual enterprise.

2. Acme Transport is a fictitious name for an actual enterprise.

Chapter 7

1. This approach was articulated in the MIT master's thesis work by Francisco Zini (2012) and Matias Raby (2012), drawing from the literature in management science.

2. There are numerous techniques for generating creative ideas—traditional brainstorming, use of metaphor, lateral thinking, and many others. The choice of any particular technique should depend, to some degree, on the culture of the enterprise. The choice of actual technique does not matter so long as it works well for the team. Techniques and environments can enable the architecting team to think outside established patterns—for example, by venturing outside the conference room for this session. Another approach is to think about a concept that is radically different than the present enterprise. To stretch the imagination, developing concepts that are vastly different is a good idea, followed by shuffling wild ideas into groupings that work well together to create alternatives.

3. Eberhardt Rechtin, *Systems Architecting of Organizations: Why Eagles Can't Swim* (Boca Raton, FL: CRC Press, 2000), 12. Note that Rechtin uses the term *complex organizations* rather than *enterprises*.

4. Collaboration for Wellness Center (CWC) is a fictitious name for an actual enterprise.

Chapter 8

1. Donna H. Rhodes, Adam M. Ross, and Deborah J. Nightingale, "Architecting the System of Systems Enterprise: Enabling Constructs and Methods from the Field of Engineering Systems," paper presented at the Third Annual IEEE Systems Conference, Vancouver, Canada, March 2009.

2. Ivan Electronics Corporation (IEC) is a fictitious name for a real-world corporation.

3. Christopher Glazner, "Understanding Enterprise Behavior Using Hybrid Simulation of Enterprise Architecture," doctoral dissertation, MIT, 2009.

4. The use of system dynamics models in enterprise architecting is demonstrated in two recent master's theses: James R. Enos, "A New Glide Path: Re-Architecting the Flight School XXI Enterprise at the U.S. Army Aviation Center of Excellence," master of science in engineering and management thesis, MIT, 2010, and James E. Richards, "Integrating the Army Geospatial Enterprise: Synchronizing Geospatial-Intelligence to the Dismounted Solder," master of science in engineering and management thesis, MIT, 2010.

5. Some architecting teams choose to add the ratings same, better, or worse. The method does not require this; it is important to recognize that the sum represents a qualitative assessment.

6. Matias Raby, "Architecting the Future Enterprise: A Framework for Supporting Decision Making in the Selection of Future States," master of science in engineering and management thesis, MIT, 2012.

7. For example, the Software Engineering Institute's Architecture Tradeoff Analysis Method (ATAM), as discussed in Luke C. G. Cropsey, "Integrating Military Unmanned Aircraft into the National Airspace System: An Application of Value-Focused Thinking and Enterprise Architecting," master of science in engineering and management thesis, MIT, 2008.

Chapter 9

1. The importance of conceptual integrity was introduced by Frederick P. Brooks in Frederick P. Brooks, *The Mythical Man-Month* (Reading, MA: Addison-Wesley, 1975).

2. Dov Dori, *Object-Process Methodology: A Holistic Systems Paradigm* (New York: Springer, 2002).

3. Mark W. Maier and Eberhardt Rechtin, *The Art of Systems Architecting*, 2nd ed. (Boca Raton, FL: CRC Press, 2000).

4. Many enterprise architecture frameworks are in wide use. A website maintained by the EABOK community and hosted by The MITRE Corporation provides foundational knowledge on enterprise architecture (http://www2.mitre.org/public/eabok). The international standard, ISO/IEC/IEEE 42010, *Systems and Software Engineering—Architecture Description,*

defines an architecture framework as "conventions, principles and practices for the description of architectures established within a specific domain of application and/or community of stakeholders". A survey of enterprise architecture frameworks is found on the website for this standard (http://www.iso-architecture.org/42010).

Chapter 10

1. LM Devices and SynCo Group are fictitious names for actual enterprises that were the subject of this study. This case includes selected excerpts from the full enterprise architecting project.

Index